WHEELS

New Russell models in front of Toronto City Hall, 1905.
Russells were Canada's first successful automobiles.

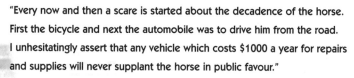

"Every now and then a scare is started about the decadence of the horse. First the bicycle and next the automobile was to drive him from the road. I unhesitatingly assert that any vehicle which costs $1000 a year for repairs and supplies will never supplant the horse in public favour."

E. King Dodds, Canadian Turf Recollections, 1910

WHEELS
The Car in Canada

DESMOND MORTON

Umbrella Press
TORONTO

To Charles and Christian St. Louis, who will carry their experience of "Wheels" well into the twenty-first century.

Publisher: Ken Pearson
Editor: Jocelyn Smyth
Special Editorial Contributor: Arlene Chan
Design: Judie Shore

Cover: A 1932 Cadillac (photo courtesy of General Motors) and a watercolour painting of a service garage. (by Don Brown) The illustrated wheel on the back cover portrays changes in the design of automobile wheels through the years. (by Dan Kangas)

Umbrella Press acknowledges the financial support of the Government of Canada through the Canadian Studies Program, (Department of) Canadian Heritage.

Canadian Cataloguing in Publication Data

Morton, Desmond, 1937–

    Wheels: the car in Canada
Includes bibliographical references and index.
ISBN 1-895642-03-5

1. Automobiles - Canada - History. 2. Automobiles - Social aspects - Canada. I Title.

TL26.M67 1998   388.3'42'0971   98-930408-6

A Three Panes and a Star Publication

Manufactured in Canada

Umbrella Press

56 Rivercourt Blvd.
Toronto ON. M4J 3A4
Telephone: (416) 696-6665
Fax: (416) 696-9189
E-mail: umbpress@interlog.com

Manitoba Archives, Foote Collection, N2736

CONTENTS

1911 Everitt made by the Tudhope Motor Company of Canada

INTRODUCTION

There are lots of ways to see history. Political change is an obvious one. Most people who are interested in the past can usually associate events with the time when Brian Mulroney or Pierre Elliott Trudeau or John Diefenbaker was in power. It is also possible, though more difficult, to remember similar social and economic events. When times get tough and unemployment increases, many people want to compare the current problems to the Great Depression of the 1930s or to the series of "recessions" since 1945. One historian developed a theory of change based on great epidemics. When the young get restless, we remember the rebellious era of the 1960s. A more cheerful approach links change to the neckline of women's dresses. That may serve the fashion-conscious, but others may regard it as a bit eccentric.

As an alternative to politics, though, fashion has an appeal. So do cars. Automobiles have been a growing feature of Canadian life and history for the past century. They began to matter in the first decade of the twentieth century and their end, if sometimes predicted, is not yet.

The automobile illuminates many aspects of Canadian economic and social history. Consider Sir John A. Macdonald's National Policy of 1879. High tariffs, Macdonald promised, would create jobs in Canada. Did it work? Historians may never agree. But look at how adding 35 per cent to the cost of any imported carriage affected Canada's own carriage builders. And remember that a car was the same as a carriage in the tariff schedule. All at once the Old Chieftain, as admirers called Macdonald, became the founder of Canada's enormous auto industry. He also ensured that the industry would be based on assembly plants controlled by foreign companies.

Automobiles shaped Canadian towns, cities and countryside. Look at a map of your city before, say, 1914. Then see how it developed by 1930 and by 1990. Imagine living without gas stations, garages and parking lots. Without cars, our vast suburbs would be unlivable. Meeting the costly needs of cars for highways and bridges forced the provinces to seek more power in Canada's federal system. In 1867, Ottawa's control of canals and railways gave it absolute control of national transportation. Who cared at that point if provinces were responsible for the few muddy roads? What a difference the car made as manufacturing it became the most important industry of Canada's richest province.

The car has affected the way Canadians live, from tourism and shopping to the way men and women get to know each other. Satisfying the car has produced vast new industries, from petroleum production and distribution to the auto insurance business. While most people a century ago had little fear of the police, everyone behind a wheel has become a potential law-breaker. Finding space for highways, roads and parking lots has created a demanding new competitor for the land we need for homes, businesses, farming and nature itself. Cars have affected the environment, from their exhaust emissions to their ultimate disposal at a junkyard. The changing shape and size of the car have affected the steel industry, plastics, rubber and glass.Only space and imagination set the limits on the theme.

The car as we know it — a passenger vehicle with a gasoline engine and four rubber tires — is just over a hundred years old, but the idea of a "horseless carriage" is much older. Automobile is a French word, and the first was a steam-powered tractor designed by a French army captain, Nicholas Cugnot, in the era of Napoleon.

The main advances in car design occurred elsewhere, mainly in France and Germany. While many designers thought that steam or electricity would be the best power source, the German engineer Niklaus Otto found the most popular answer when he designed a four-stroke gasoline-powered engine. Two other Germans, Gottfried Daimler and Wilhelm Maybach, managed to adapt the Otto engine for use in a car. A French engineer, Emile Levassor, solved the problem of the auto frame which holds the engine, body and wheels together. In 1886, Karl Benz made the first successful car with an internal-combustion engine. Benz named it after a shareholder's daughter, Mercedes. Many of the world's great luxury cars still bear the name of Mercedes Benz.

Adventurous people were attracted to automobiles, but thousands of inventions were needed before cars could be safe and reliable. Imagine the difficulty of designing dependable steering, brakes, transmissions, suspension systems, even the instruments and lighting. Americans made the big strides in turning a huge toy for the rich into a low-priced convenience for most people. "Mass production" began with Ransom E. Olds and his Oldsmobile. Detroit and its neighbouring communities had become famous as a centre for building carriages, and car-making was the natural next step. And just across the Detroit River was Canada.

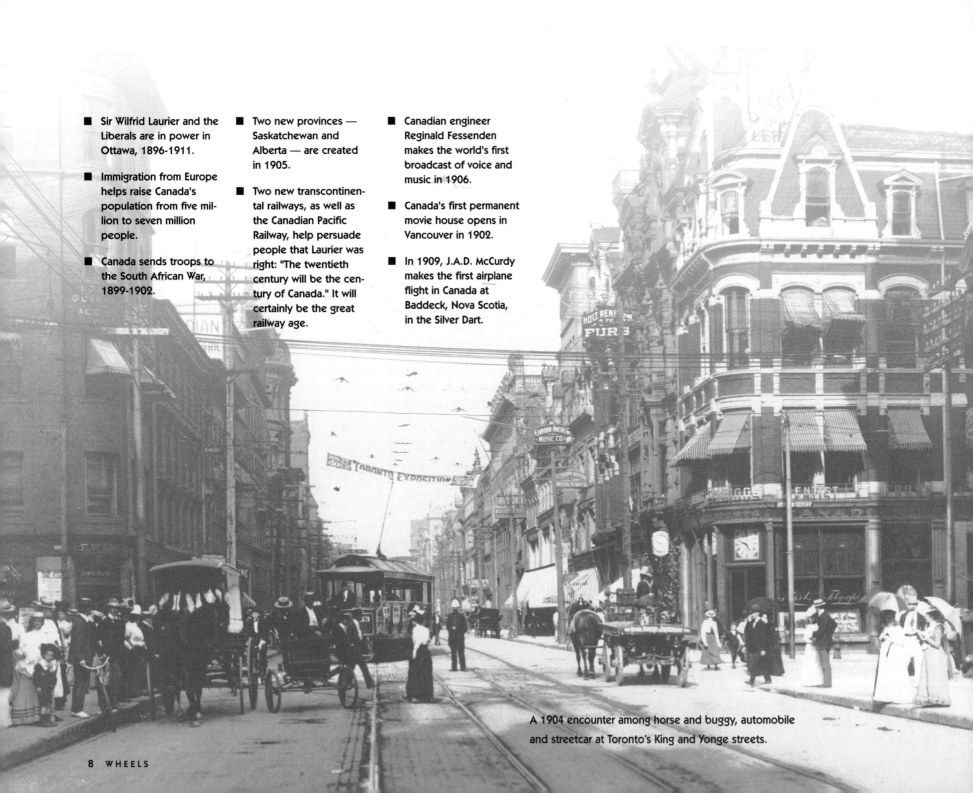

- Sir Wilfrid Laurier and the Liberals are in power in Ottawa, 1896-1911.

- Immigration from Europe helps raise Canada's population from five million to seven million people.

- Canada sends troops to the South African War, 1899-1902.

- Two new provinces — Saskatchewan and Alberta — are created in 1905.

- Two new transcontinental railways, as well as the Canadian Pacific Railway, help persuade people that Laurier was right: "The twentieth century will be the century of Canada." It will certainly be the great railway age.

- Canadian engineer Reginald Fessenden makes the world's first broadcast of voice and music in 1906.

- Canada's first permanent movie house opens in Vancouver in 1902.

- In 1909, J.A.D. McCurdy makes the first airplane flight in Canada at Baddeck, Nova Scotia, in the Silver Dart.

A 1904 encounter among horse and buggy, automobile and streetcar at Toronto's King and Yonge streets.

CHAPTER ONE

1900-1910

AUTO AND INDUSTRY-MAKERS

In the 1900s, most Canadians got around by horse and buggy, street car or on foot. If they travelled far, they went by train. In the 1890s, a bicycle craze had sent thousands of young men and women whizzing into the countryside, only to return weary, dusty and muddy from the few crude tracks that served country people as roads.

Crazes pass. By the 1900s, Canadians were looking at a new one, the "horseless carriage." The idea was not new. In 1867, the year Canada was born, a watchmaker in Stanstead, Quebec, named Henry Seth Taylor had built a "steam pleasure palace" on wheels. It took him seven years to finish the job. Like most new ideas, it had not caught on. One reason was that Taylor had not really solved two tough problems. His steam engine was hot and dangerous, and we would think it was terribly slow — so slow that he didn't install brakes. And that was his second problem. One day, his "pleasure palace" started rolling down hill. Taylor jumped for his life, but his car was smashed beyond repair.

Henry Seth Taylor's "steam pleasure palace"

By the 1890s, lots of engineers had produced self-propelled vehicles, or to use the fashionable French word, automobiles. Most looked like a one-horse buggy, with a little engine stuck on the back or front. Lots of people knew how to build a carriage, and automobile makers were soon producing nice glistening ones, complete with mudguards, a canopy and a shiny dashboard. Some even included a holder for the buggy whip. Which engine — steam, electric or "gasolene" — was best? A gasoline-powered engine, invented by Niklaus Otto and perfected in Germany by Gottfried Daimler, took years to emerge as the most successful. Another problem was the chassis, the framework that holds the wheels and the spring. The best designs came from France, where smart mechanics figured out the best way to transmit power from the motor to the axle and wheels, and how to arrange the steering so that the car could change direction without turning over. One of the first successful cars was made in Germany in 1886 by Karl Benz, who named it for his daughter, Mercedes. The name survives for one of the world's best-known luxury cars.

Often, it is not who dreams up a good idea but who gets it into production that matters. In that race, Americans were the winners. By 1900, an American, Ransom E. Olds, had figured out the basic principles of mass production with his Oldsmobile. Henry Ford, a bicycle mechanic from Dearborn, Michigan, surpassed Olds by producing replaceable parts and using conveyor belts to carry cars and parts past workers who did some bit of the assembly job and passed it on to a neighbour. By doing the same job over and over and over again, assembly workers got more skilful and a whole lot faster. Assembly-line techniques helped make Ford a multi-millionaire.

Back in 1879, as part of his famous job-creating "National Policy," Canada's prime minister, Sir John A. Macdonald, had slapped a tariff of 35 percent on imported carriages. That meant that a Canadian buyer would save money by choosing a $530 Canadian-made carriage, horseless or not, over a $400 American-built carriage (though only if the Canadian vehicle worked!) A Canadian carriage industry prospered, and most cities and towns had a few factories, each with a few dozen workers.

In 1897, the Canadian Motor Syndicate was formed to back William Still, an electrician who wanted to use his new, improved storage battery to drive a carriage. By the 1900s, several Canadian factories were wrestling with the problems of making horseless carriages. If batteries at the turn of the century had been strong and dependable, Still's syndicate would have chosen a winner. They didn't: their little battery-powered car reached a speed of 20 kilometres an hour, but it could only run for an hour. Nor did the people who backed Oland Brooks's steam-powered car. Some people were smarter — or luckier. Since the problems of making a good car were big, it made sense to look to people who had already solved them, notably in England and the United States.

above: **In 1897, Dr. H. Casgrain of Quebec City purchased Canada's first gasoline-motor vehicle, an imported Bollée Voiturette, for $600. Dr. and Mrs. Casgrain are seen here the following February, when the motor tricycle had been fitted with runners for winter driving.**

left: **William Still in 1898 with a gasolene car he developed after his earlier electric models.**

Gordon McGregor of the Walkerville Wagon Works and his foreman, Wallace R. Campbell, saw the obvious solution. In 1904, they began ferrying chassis and motors across the Detroit River from Henry Ford's new automobile factory. That way, they sneaked Ford's efficient designs into Canada without the 35 percent tariff. In October, 1904, McGregor drove the first Model C Ford down Windsor's main street.

above: **At the turn of the century, "wheels" meant bicycles. One Canadian in 12 had one, and few believed that cars would ever be more than a rich man's toy.** National Archives of Canada, C39096

left: **Early cars were notoriously unreliable, a fact that carriage makers like the McLaughlins took obvious delight in pointing out, at least until they got into the automobile business themselves.**

Ford himself noticed something else. In 1897, Sir Wilfrid Laurier's new Liberal government had introduced "imperial preference" — lower tariffs for trade within a British Empire that spanned the world. Great Britain and other colonies and dominions responded. Having bought the Walkerville factory, Ford let it sell cars anywhere in the Empire except England and Ireland where he had already built his own factory. Ford had another idea. Like a lot of bosses, he wanted his employees to be loyal and obedient, but he also wanted them to earn enough to buy his product. That meant high wages — five dollars a day by 1914 — and the cheapest possible cars.

From the Tudhopes at Orillia, Ontario, to the McKays in Kentville, Nova Scotia, lots of Canadians tried their hand at making cars in the 1900s. In 1910, the census reported ten factories with 2438 employees. Their common problem was that, without borrowing American know-how, every problem had to be solved from scratch. So they borrowed. Sam McLaughlin was typical. In Oshawa, his father had built up one of the biggest carriage-building businesses in Canada.

In 1908, Sam decided to forget about horses. He made a deal with the founding genius of General Motors, William C. Durant, and began installing David Buick's American-built engines.

CANADA'S FIRST TRAFFIC FATALITY

Winnipeg claims the dubious honour of registering Canada's first traffic victim, city resident James Lougheed. The accident happened on May 1, 1900, and was very much of the day: Lougheed was killed when his horse, frightened by an electric car, bolted and threw him out of his buggy.

The McLaughlin could reach 60 kilometres an hour on its 22-horsepower engine, and it sold for $1420 — as much as a school principal earned at the time. When his operation thrived, he decided to buy the rights to the "Classic Six," a five-passenger car designed by racing driver Louis Chevrolet. Soon McLaughlin and Chevrolet had formed General Motors of Canada, or GMC. The result was a better car at a lower price, more jobs for his home town — and, of course, a bigger profit for "Colonel Sam."

above: **Dirt roads became muddy quagmires in wet weather.**
left: **Early motoring costumes were designed for dusty roads.**
Canadian Automobile Museum

Russell

Switching from carriages to cars seemed logical, but there were problems. Carriage-builders accepted tolerances as loose as a sixteenth of an inch (1.5 mm) and few of them did much work in metal. Bicycle-builders were a lot closer in technology. Canada Cycle and Motor (CCM), the big winners in the bicycle boom, decided to make high quality their main selling point. Their Russell motor cars, said the advertisements, were "made up to a standard, not down to a price." The cheapest model, a tiny two-cylinder run-about, cost $1500; the top-of-the-line, a seven-passenger, 50-horse-power gas-guzzler, cost $4500. At the time, a skilled mechanic might earn up to $800 a year; the prime minister of Canada was paid $7000. Russell depended on the Dodge Brothers for its technology. Without a mass market and proud of their skilled workers, Russell, McLaughlin and Tudhope all boasted of the high-quality finish of their cars. McLaughlin's version of the Buick featured East African mahogany, a black moulded roof from England and leather and wool upholstery.

Governments began counting cars as soon as they had figured out how to tax them. Ontario started in 1903, and in 1905 it ordered drivers to paint the licence number on the car. British Columbia caught up with the counting in 1907, reporting 175 motor vehicles in the province. In 1908, eight Canadian provinces reported a total of 3033 cars; the ninth province, tiny, rural Prince Edward Island, simply banned them as smelly, dangerous and unnecessary. Five years later, the Island had a change of heart: automobiles would be allowed out on Mondays, Tuesdays and Thursdays, but rural townships could still ban them if they preferred.

GEORGE FOSS

Born in Sherbrooke, Quebec, Foss is credited with driving the first gasoline-powered automobile in Canada. Before Foss every automobile built in Canada had been either electric or steam powered, but was much too impractical for everyday use. Foss designed and built his automobile himself. It had many special features, including a front-mounted, air-cooled engine with a single cylinder, four-cycle system. He drove it in all seasons, which was unusual at that time. Later, he secured the Canadian rights for the Crestmobile, which was built in Cambridge, Massachusetts, and took a position as an automobile salesman. In later years Foss opened a machine shop in Montreal and started that city's first fast car wash.

Canadian Automobile Museum

LICENCES

In 1903, Ontario became the first province to issue car licences. These were patent leather plaques with aluminum numbers. At the time, other provinces issued individual motorists with a number for their car and left it to the motorists to make their own plates, usually out of wood, metal or leather. One defiant car owner used a broomstick as the indicator for his licence — number 1.

top: New 1902 models being delivered to the Automobile and Supply Company on King Street East in Toronto.

ONTARIO SPEED LIMITS

When Ontario decided to set a speed limit for automobiles in 1903, it proposed 8 miles (13 km) per hour in the city. This was upped to 10 miles (16 km) after much argument by the Toronto Automobile Club and test rides by all elected members of the provincial legislature.

That speed limit — along with 15 mph (24 km/h) in open country — remained in effect until 1912. Finally, after long and persistent complaining by motorists, the legislature allowed motor vehicles to be driven as fast as 15 mph (24 km/h) in the city and 20 mph (32 km/h) in open country.

By 1919, there had been such an increase in the number of cars (and consequently in the number of voters who wanted to drive them faster) that the limit was raised to 20 mph (32 km/h) for cities and 25 mph (40 km/h) for country driving.

The "Every Day" Car

The Car for Service

CAN BE OPERATED EVERY DAY IN THE YEAR

No Tire Troubles

$ 650 Fully Equipped $

6
5
0

above: Factory scene at the turn of the century. Today, much of the work on the assembly line is done by robotics.

left: The Tudhope had no doors or windshield but was "fully equipped" with lamps and a top. It was produced by the Woodstock Automobile Manufacturing Company of Woodstock Ontario.

Since 1853, the old United Canada's had a Highway Travel Act that required vehicles to keep to the right, pass on the left and forbade drunks to ride or drink. Racing, "furious driving" or shouting and using "blasphemous or indecent language" could be punished by a fine or a month in jail. Ontario adopted a Traction Engines Act in 1868 which limited the big machines to six miles an hour (or 10 km/h) and required them to be led by a messenger with a red flag in daytime and a red lantern at night. In the early years of the automobile, towns and cities passed hundreds of different regulations. In 1903, Ontario tried to bring order out of chaos with a new Motor Vehicles Act. The speed limit would be 16 km/h in built up areas and 24 km/h elsewhere, but drivers had to slow down to avoid frightening horses. Cars needed headlamps and a proper "alarm bell, gong or horn" — still the rule 85 years later.

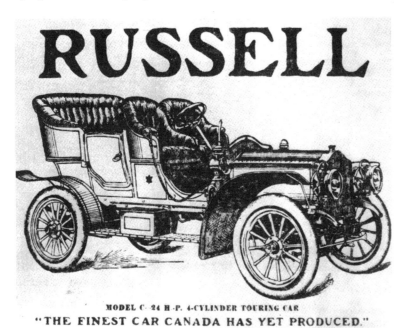

RUSSELL

MODEL C- 24 H.-P. 4-CYLINDER TOURING CAR
"THE FINEST CAR CANADA HAS YET PRODUCED."

The sales of this model during the Show have been greater than any other Car. **There Must be a Reason.** | Local Representatives : Canada Cycle & Motor Co., Ltd., Dominion Automobile Co. Toronto Junction.

For the most part, Canada's earliest motorists bought their gasoline in cans or buckets from the neighbourhood grocery or hardware store. The first filling station opened in Vancouver in 1907. Located beside the Imperial Oil warehouse, it was originally just a three-sided shed open to the street. A converted water tank held the gasoline, which was transferred to cars through a garden hose. Seen here is the expanded station as it was in 1912. Imperial Oil Archives

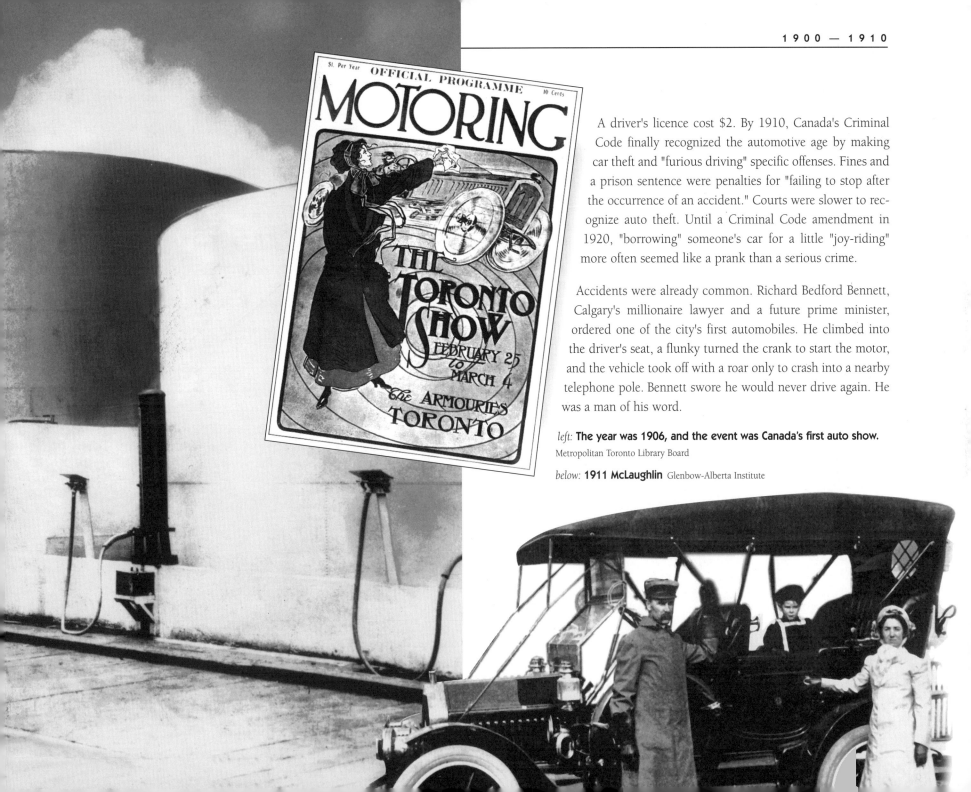

$1 Per Year **OFFICIAL PROGRAMME** 10 Cents

MOTORING

THE TORONTO SHOW

FEBRUARY 25 to MARCH 4

The ARMOURIES TORONTO

A driver's licence cost $2. By 1910, Canada's Criminal Code finally recognized the automotive age by making car theft and "furious driving" specific offenses. Fines and a prison sentence were penalties for "failing to stop after the occurrence of an accident." Courts were slower to recognize auto theft. Until a Criminal Code amendment in 1920, "borrowing" someone's car for a little "joy-riding" more often seemed like a prank than a serious crime.

Accidents were already common. Richard Bedford Bennett, Calgary's millionaire lawyer and a future prime minister, ordered one of the city's first automobiles. He climbed into the driver's seat, a flunky turned the crank to start the motor, and the vehicle took off with a roar only to crash into a nearby telephone pole. Bennett swore he would never drive again. He was a man of his word.

left: **The year was 1906, and the event was Canada's first auto show.**
Metropolitan Toronto Library Board

below: **1911 McLaughlin** Glenbow-Alberta Institute

- Sir Robert Borden is prime minister in a Conservative government, 1911 to 1921.

- Over 40 00 immigrants enter Canada in 1913.

- Women in Manitoba, Saskatchewan and Alberta win the right to vote in provincial elections in 1916.

- 600 000 Canadians enlist to serve in the First World War; 60 000 never return.

- Federal income tax is introduced as a temporary wartime measure in 1917. It is still collected.

- In 1917, an explosion aboard a French munitions ship in Halifax harbour destroys much of the city.

- In 1918, Canadian women finally win the right to vote in federal elections.

- Both the new transcontinental railways slide into bankruptcy; the government takes them over and creates the Canadian National Railways.

BEFORE WINDSHIELD WIPERS

The following helpful hint was offered to motorists in 1913: "To keep your windshield clear of mist on rainy days, rub a sliced onion over the glass with an up and down motion. This will be found to be an admirable protection against rain obscuring the vision."

By the end of the decade, cars were an everyday part of the city street scene. It would be a while yet, however, before they did not have to share the road with horse-drawn wagons.

City of Toronto Archives, James 492

CHAPTER TWO

1910-1920

HIGHWAY AND NATION BUILDERS

By 1914, Henry Ford had managed to chop the price of his Model T down to $490. That put it within the buying power of a prosperous farmer with a good crop and a mechanical bent. Many fathers soon found that their sons were more expert in "gapping" a spark plug or engaging the gears without a gust of jack-rabbit starts. The Model T fitted a lot of needs in the 1910s. The body was slung high enough for the ruts in rural roads, the local blacksmith could probably hammer out a spare part or two, and a team of horses could rescue the "Tin Lizzie" from most mishaps.

Given the state of Canada's roads, mishaps were frequent. Neglected because of two generations of railway building, most were primitive dirt tracks that just allowed a farmer to haul produce to the nearest railway line. In much of Canada, they were no more than logging trails.

A few improved roads had been built by private companies, with authority from provincial legislatures to charge tolls. Outside Ottawa, the Aylmer and Bytown Turnpike Co. decided that automobiles would pay the same rate as carriages. Local motorists complained that the nineteenth-century laws authorizing tolls made no mention of cars. A.M. McKay of the Ottawa Motor Transport Co. forced the issue by smashing a toll gate with his two-ton truck. McKay won the case.

1915 Model T Ford. Even at $1150 in 1909, the first Model T had been a great success and their price continued to go down as their sales increased — to $750 by 1912 and to about $400 for the very basic ones by the mid-1920s. The last were produced in 1926.

Windsor Star

Now that more farmers owned cars — or wanted them — they provided the political muscle for "Good Roads" associations. Even Prince Edward Island's farmer relented: by 1918, cars could be driven seven days a week. In major cities, drivers formed auto clubs. Once they had sent out scouts to map the roads and put up direction signs, they joined the campaign for better roads. In 1913 a national Good Roads Association and the Canadian Automobile Association were formed to lobby Ottawa. True, the British North America Act had left "Local Works and Undertakings" such as roads to the provinces; but that was when they hardly mattered. Robert Borden's new Conservative government, eager to oblige, twice tried to get national highways legislation through Parliament. Each time the Senate had a sober second thought and the law failed to pass.

top: **Makeshift traffic sign, 1912.** City of Toronto Archives, James 9158

right: **Learning the hard way about the hazards of winter driving.** City of Toronto Archives, James 1575

Driving could be complicated. Here are the directions for starting an early car:

- Pull out the choke;
- Retard the spark lever;
- Advance the throttle;
- Turn the ignition switch;
- Climb out;
- Turn the crank until the engine fires;
- Race back to the driver's seat;
- Advance the spark;
- Switch to magneto;
- Slowly push in the choke.

The outbreak of the Great War in August 1914 prevented a third try, but automotive production boomed. In 1914, Canadian factories produced 14 000 cars and trucks (or "freight automobiles" as they were called). By 1917, output reached 94 000. Cars were a reward that a wartime profiteer (and his wife) could enjoy. So could farmers. In the name of progress and efficiency, governments urged farmers to acquire tractors. Most farmers still preferred horses for farm work, and for the $1200 spent on a Bates Steel Mule, they could buy three teams and have cash left over. A car could take the family to town in style. "The day you buy an automobile," said the *Farm and Ranch Review*, "it will pick your farm right up and drop it two-thirds nearer the religious, social and market centres."

above: **Model F Galts stuck in the snow on their way to the showrooms. The company boasted that the electric starter system would work in any conditions. Unfortunately, it was, in fact, unreliable and gained a poor reputation.**

LICENCE PLATES

Provinces began to issue their own licence plates before the First World War. Ontario was the first province to issue licences when a bill was passed in 1903 requiring all automobile owners to pay the fee of $2.00 for each vehicle.

In 1911, Quebec, Manitoba and New Brunswick issued their plates, followed in 1912 by Alberta and Saskatchewan and in 1913 by British Columbia. Nova Scotia didn't issue licences until 1918 and it wasn't until 1923 that the Yukon issued them. At first in Prince Edward Island the government issued a number and allowed the owner to make a plate. In 1918 the government began issuing its own plates.

At the end of the first trans-Canada trip, October 18, 1912, Thomas Wilby empties a bottle of Atlantic water into the Pacific.

TIRES

In 1912 the average cost of a tire was $50. This was exceeding high, particularly as tires were always being punctured by stones and horseshoe nails on the roads. By the time a tire had traveled 3000 miles (4800 km) it was usually too worn for use and had to be replaced. Initially, tires were perfectly smooth, with no tread, but by 1910 non-skid treads were introduced.

Between 1910 and 1930 or so, over 50 different makes of Canadian cars were produced in dozens of towns and cities scattered from Lethbridge, Alberta, to Amherst, Nova Scotia, and Saint John, New Brunswick. Like most of the cars at the turn of the century this 1913 "McKay" was either a five-passenger touring car or a roadster, and in either case the car was open.

BODY STYLES

After 1910 the standard body styles were the five-passenger touring car and the two-passenger roadster. It wasn't until the 1920s that the rumble seat was added at the back of the car. At first the automobiles were open style for everyone except the very rich, but as driving in the winter became more common, the cars were closed.

GASOLINE ENGINE

By 1910 the gasoline car became the standard, and it continues to this day. It included the engine in the front of the car, the transmission behind it, and a shaft drive to the rear axle. In recent years, however, the front-wheel drive has become common. A major breakthrough for the gasoline engine in Canada was the introduction of the electric self-starter in 1912. Previously, the engine had to be cranked by hand, which was both dangerous and virtually impossible for women. The first successful electric starter was introduced in the Cadillac in the United States the previous year.

below: **The quest for an energy- and cost-efficient electric car has been ongoing since we began driving mechanical vehicles. The Model C Peck followed CCM's Ivanhoe model and was displayed at the 1912 Toronto show. Alas, it was short lived as the electric starter, and its high price, doomed it.**

On July 26, 1913, Bob Burman set a Canadian speed record of one mile (1.6 km) in 50.8 seconds in his Blitzen Benz. Imperial Oil Archives

Service station, 1916
Imperial Oil Archives

The ELECTRIC CAR
FOR CANADA

Because the Peck is built in Canada, which gives with your purchase assurance of factory service, eliminates repair worries and saves custom duties.

Because it has more superior points of difference than any other electric car made.

1.—The steering gear is absolute frictionless.

2.—The foot control allows an instant stop or gradual acceleration to the speed required.

3.—Brakes are absolutely true. The Peck hand brake lever opens the armature circuit making it impossible to lock the car, and leave power on.

4.—The steering mast can be adjusted to the sitting posture of the user.

There are 100 other features, but the symetrical graceful lines; the deep hand built upholstering; the exquisite finish, and its ease of operation and ready charging are best seen.

Peck Electric Coupe Model "C" demonstrates the long-wanted combination of high quality and moderate price. From every point—it represents the highest point reached in electric car building . . . $4,000

At a telephone call, we call for—charge—wash—and deliver cars—for which we make the modest charge of $30 per month

"KEEPS PECKING"

Peck ELECTRIC

As wartime prices gave them the best years most of them could remember, prairie farmers bought automobiles at a rate unmatched anywhere else in the country. Soldiers, coming home from the war, pointed to cars as proof that the war had done very well for Canadians. By 1919, 341 316 cars were registered across the country. Prince Edward Island, which had begun with 50 cars in 1916, boasted 1250 by 1919. Ontario led with 144 804.

Most cars had to be started by a hand crank — heavy work, miserable in cold and wet weather and dangerous if the crank jumped back, breaking the odd finger and occasional arm. An electric starter, devised by Cadillac in 1912 "to make driving a pleasure ladies could enjoy," was a comfort to men too.

Soldiers had seen a lot of motor vehicles in the army. Horses still hauled most of the guns, ammunition and supplies, but Colonel Sam Hughes, Canada's wartime Minister of Militia, was a convert to the new fad. He bought Model T's for his staff officers, boasting that they were cheap enough to throw away if they broke down. The Canadian Expeditionary Force sailed with cars and trucks of almost every known make as Hughes set out to publicize Canada's proudest new industry. More enthusiastic than knowledgeable, Hughes never did grasp the problems of providing thousands of spare parts for each different model of car and truck.

Few of Hughes's new cars and trucks ever left England, but the armoured trucks of the Canadian Motor Machine Gun Brigade fought throughout the war and especially in 1918. By then, rigid lines of trenches were broken and armoured trucks could race machine guns to stop an enemy attack.

Canada used mechanized support for the first time during warfare. Canadian-made motor cars and trucks were expected to win world markets. In practice, most vehicles broke down in English conditions. National Archives of Canada, PA C11264

A shipment of Canadian-made armoured cars reached the North-West frontier between India and Afghanistan, and served for years after the war. Overseas, thousands of Canadian men and women learned to drive and service the army's cars, trucks and ambulances. When they came home, veterans lined up for courses on motor mechanics. The Military Hospitals Commission argued that a transcontinental highway, built by unemployed veterans, would be a magnificent Canadian war memorial.

In 1919, the federal government finally got a highway act through the Senate. It offered $20 million to be shared among the provinces for roads that not only met high standards of construction but could be linked up in a trans-Canada highway. Most provinces needed no reminder that they had entered the automotive age. Even during wartime labour shortages that made it difficult to bring in the harvest, Ontario had kept gangs of workers labouring on Highway No. 2 linking Toronto to Hamilton and, ultimately, to the American border. Provinces followed Ontario's lead in regulating drivers. British Columbia's Motor Vehicle Act was typical. It banned drivers under seventeen, set speed limits of 15 miles (24 km) an hour in towns, cities and wooded areas, and allowed "scorchers" to race at twice that speed in the open country.

opposite: **Women volunteers take over the gas pumps during the Winnipeg General Strike, 1919.** Manitoba Archives, Foote Collection, N2736

below: **A wartime driver in the First World War changes the tire on her Canadian Red Cross ambulance.** National Archives of Canada, PA 1249

- William Lyon Mackenzie King and the Liberals are in power between 1921 and 1930, except for a brief Conservative interlude.

- Canadians have their first experience of radio broadcasting.

- The Group of Seven gives Canadians a special look at their land.

- Canada's first registered airport (called an "air harbour") opens in Regina in 1920.

- In 1921, four medical researchers at the University of Toronto discover insulin as a therapy for diabetics.

- Regular airmail service begins in 1924.

- Pioneer aviators help open the north.

- The Royal Canadian Air Force is established in 1924.

- In 1927, the Old Age Pension Plan is introduced.

- In the "Persons" case, British judges overrule Canada's Supreme Court and decide that women are "persons" too and can, therefore, sit in the Senate of Canada.

- American businesses begin investing massively in Canada, creating big branch plants.

Douglas Kemp went to work in the paint shop at McLaughlin's in 1927. His job was preparing auto bodies before they were sprayed. He sanded, buffed, filled holes and smoothed wood on 17 to 18 cars an hour, keeping up the company's high standards of finish. His pay was two cents a car. In his first year he earned $1000, enough to buy himself a second-hand 1923 touring car.

An early assembly of a complicated machine was a North American triumph. It meant that a car was a luxury most families could eventually afford. Author's Collection

CHAPTER THREE

1920-1930

ROAD USERS

The 1920s put Canadians on wheels. Only the United States out-ranked Canada as a world producer, exporter and owner of cars. Of the 203 307 automobiles that rolled out of Canadian factories in 1929, 64 683 left the country as exports. So did half the 59 319 buses and trucks. Imperial preference guided most of them to Australia, New Zealand, South Africa and India, but there were buyers in Argentina, Chile, Norway and half a dozen other countries. The disastrous 1923 Yokohama earthquake knocked out the region's auto industry and helped open Japan as a new market for Canadian trucks.

Enough motor vehicles were left over to provide a car for every ten Canadians. British Columbia's ratio, one car for every seven people, was a better proof of that province's new resource wealth than any chamber of commerce could devise. Cars in the 1920s were cheaper and better too, with roofs, steel bodies, mudguards, electric lights, glass side-windows, windshield wipers, a gas gauge and "balloon tires" that somehow managed to survive most trips without a puncture.

The innovations were mostly American. The branch-plant invasion transformed Canada's auto industry. In 1920, there were seventeen factories; only ten survived the decade. Chrysler came to Canada, but the Russells were gone. So was the Gray-Dort "rolling bathtub" and the Brooks Steam Car, usually because their adopted American partners had failed. A newcomer in the 1920s was Walter Chrysler, who bought up Windsor's Maxwell-Chalmers Motor Co. when it ran into trouble. In 1925, as the Chrysler Corporation of Canada, its 181 workers produced 7857 new cars. Soon, Chrysler was producing trucks in nearby Walkerville, and it would add Dodge, Desoto and Plymouth models.

The London Six, "Canada's Quality Car"

American-owned automotive plants soon stretched in a thin line from Oshawa to Windsor, close to the belching American steel mills and the scores of parts factories that kept most of the new jobs south of the border. In 1926, the government finally slashed the 35 percent tariff to only 20 percent, but it also promised deeper tariff cuts for any vehicle with more than 50 percent Canadian content. Hardly anyone now dreamed of a purely Canadian-made car, just a fairer share of the market.

Nor were Canadian manufacturers as eager as Americans to develop a mass market. The old "quality" snobbery survived. Henry Ford complained that even his own Canadian branch plant was too slow to trim its prices. Canadian consumers were not so fussy: they wanted their "wheels" at American prices. The spread of American magazines and radio across the border told them what to demand.

For most young Canadians in the 1920s, the origins of automotive technology hardly mattered. Farmers' sons, weary of working from dawn to dusk on land an older brother would inherit, flocked to the new factories. Car manufacturing was noisy, dangerous work, subject to sudden speed-ups in the assembly line when managers wanted more production. Efficiency experts with stopwatches checked on performance and weeded out the slow and inefficient workers. Most Canadian factories in the 1920s offered similar conditions, however, and there was a special glamour to building cars. here was another benefit too. Henry Ford grew increasingly mean and tyrannical, but he had pioneered high wages for his workers. If they could not afford his cars, he reasoned, he would never sell very many. His competitors had to match rates as high as a dollar an hour. Some car makers pioneered pension plans and health care for workers.

above: **Gray-Dort factory in Chatham, Ontario, 1920.**

below: **Garages and gas stations multiplied along with cars in the 1920s. This one was located in Ste-Anne-des-Chênes, Manitoba.** Manitoba Archives

GETS A CLOSE SHAVE

Among new devices for facilitating highway maintenance is the so called "road razor," which , its maker says, will "shave" the roughest of dirt roads so clean and smooth that it will resemble a boulevard. If the "razor" will do this, thousands of Canadian motorists will nominate its inventor for the hall of fame. *Globe and Mail, September 3, 1921*

During the 1920s, Canadians were busy building roads to satisfy the new passion for the automobile. Here, while traffic uses a narrow two-lane road near Oakville, Ontario, a steamroller flattens the ground for a new road and a pile driver in the background prepares the footing for a new bridge.

City of Toronto Archives, James 9150

ONTARIO SUPREME IN MOTOR LIST

Below are given the latest returns from the different Provinces in Canada for motor vehicle registrations in the year 1920. These figures do not include motorcycles, which number in the thousands, but do include trucks.

Nearly one-third of the cars in the Dominion are operated in Ontario. There are as may cars in this Province as in all the territory in Canada west from Fort Frances to the Pacific Coast, and two and a half times as many cars as in Eastern Canada from the Quebec border to the Atlantic Coast in the Maritime Provinces.

Ontario	172 065
Saskatchewan	60 325
Quebec	43 450
Alberta	37 515
Manitoba	36 455
British Columbia	28 136
Nova Scotia	12 456
New Brunswick	11 101
PE Island	1 426
Total in Canada	402 929

In the 1920s, the car and its attendants were everywhere. By 1923, 2500 service stations, with their boxy architecture and their pumps, dotted urban intersections and rural roadsides. Before the 1920s, Canadian cities had grown by extending narrow fingers of housing outward along existing tramways. The width of these "fingers" was decided by how far tramway commuters were willing to walk. The automobile allowed middle-class Canadians to build homes between these "fingers," creating suburban "garden communities" where poverty, crime and other big-city miseries could be left behind. Somehow the passionate urban reform crusades of the early 1900s did not look as important any more. Time once given to charity and community concerns was now needed for commuting.

left top: **Supplying car owners led to hundreds of new businesses and industries. This Winnipeg business specialized in selling, patching, retreading and rebuilding rubber tires.** Manitoba Archives, Foote Collection

bottom: **Tires were relatively expensive and a long way from being perfected, and country roads were equally primitive. Accidents were, therefore, frequent and flat tires even more so.** National Archives of Canada, PA 19348 & PA 18470

SPARE TIRES

In September 1921, the Globe offered this advice about spare tires: "It is a good plan to carry a used tire as a spare and use the newly purchased one. For a new tire held as a spare is a temptation to a thief."

ROAD CONDITIONS REPORTED IN THE NEWSPAPER IN 1921

Niagara Falls, Ontario The roads in and around Niagara Falls are in good condition this week. The Thorold road is still blocked at Collard's Corner. Go to Thorold by Lundy's Lane or by St. David's. The stone road from St. David's to St. Catharines is under repair near Homer, and there is a detour to the Niagara Stone Road.

Brampton, Ontario Motorists are complaining of damaged tires where too coarse stone has been laid on the piece of road on the Centre road, a short distance south of this town.

As usual, Quebec's response to the car was a little different. By the end of the 1920s, French-speaking Montrealers were only half as likely to own a car as their English-speaking neighbours — in fact, only half as likely as people in Winnipeg's multicultural North End. In 1931, 42 percent of Canadian farmers owned a car but only 19 percent of Quebec farmers. Poverty was not the reason: Quebec's farmers were as well (or badly) off as any others in Canada. Was it because manufacturers were out of touch with the market? Ford waited until 1914 to even produce a brochure in French. Although A.F. Lavoie's early automobile has been called "one of the very best cars that Canada ever produced," he got no backers. On the other hand, lawyer Charlie Trudeau made a fortune developing a Quebec-based chain of gas sta-

tions. His son Pierre would later become the prime minister of Canada. During the twenties, Canada probably spent more of its resources on highways than did the United States. Provinces managed to apply at least a gravel surface to 130 000 of Canada's 500 000 kilometres of roads. Why such an effort? One reason was that four provinces in the 1920s had farmer-dominated governments, whose backers wanted to get produce to market and their families to town.

Filling up at the curbside pump. Public Archives of Canada

Eaton's Model T stop light fits on any standard tail lamp. Complete with all cables and switches for $1.15.

Eaton's Catalogue, 1927.

Why go to a car wash when this "auto laundry" on the Humber River near Toronto was free? Cars in 1927 were built with a high clearance because without enough bridges, drivers sometimes had to find small rivers and streams to cross.

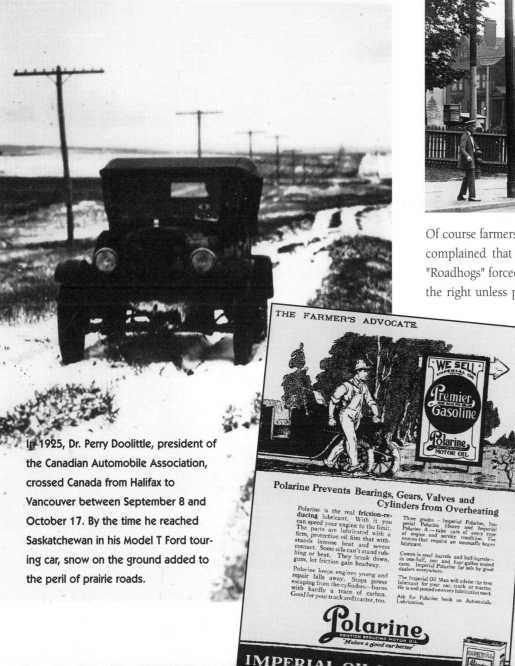

Of course farmers did not all agree about highway construction. Rural people complained that dust clouds from "speedsters" were damaging the crops. "Roadhogs" forced decent farmers into the ditch. Rules of the road — keep to the right unless passing — were not standardized in Canada until 1922-23.

Some farmers buried planks with spikes at the edge of dirt roads. One Alberta farmer "improved" a notorious slough on the Calgary-Edmonton highway — and kept a team of horses on hand to offer a little profitable help to stranded motorists. Some wanted roads for their horses and wagons, not for cars. Some resented the waste of good arable land. Rural backers of Ontario Premier Ernest Drury's farmer-labour government insisted that a single lane, with passing places and lots of 90-degree corners to respect farmers' fields, would give the province adequate highways. Drury insisted on good two-lane highways and farmers helped defeat him in 1923.

above: **A tight squeeze between an automobile and a public transit vehicle.** National Archives of Canada, PA 55051

left: **Imperial Oil ad, 1920s.** Imperial Oil Archives

In 1925, Dr. Perry Doolittle, president of the Canadian Automobile Association, crossed Canada from Halifax to Vancouver between September 8 and October 17. By the time he reached Saskatchewan in his Model T Ford touring car, snow on the ground added to the peril of prairie roads.

THE FARMER'S ADVOCATE.

WE SELL IMPERIAL OIL
Premier
MORE MILES PER GALLON
Gasoline

Polarine
MOTOR OIL

Polarine Prevents Bearings, Gears, Valves and Cylinders from Overheating

Polarine is the real friction-reducing lubricant. With it you can speed your engine to the limit. The parts are lubricated with a firm, protective oil film that withstands intense heat and severe contact. Some oils can't stand rubbing or heat. They break down, gum, let friction gain headway.

Polarine keeps engines young and repair bills away. Stops power escaping from the cylinders—burns with hardly a trace of carbon. Good for your truck and tractor, too.

Three grades – Imperial Polarine, Imperial Polarine Heavy and Imperial Polarine A – take care of every type of engine and service condition. For motors that require an unusually heavy lubricant.

Comes in steel barrels and half-barrels—in one-half, one and four-gallon sealed cans. Imperial Polarine for sale by good dealers everywhere.

The Imperial Oil Man will advise the best lubricant for your car, truck or tractor. He is well posted on every lubrication need.

Ask for Polarine book on Automobile Lubrication.

Polarine
FRICTION REDUCING MOTOR OIL
"Makes a good car better"

IMPERIAL

Attracting tourists was another road-building argument politicians could understand. As early as 1912, Montreal had been linked to the American border by a "modern highway" and soon reaped the benefits. North Americans had always been a people on the move and the car was increasingly their vehicle of choice. With the spread of paid vacations in the 1920s, sightseeing became a mass national pastime, at least for middle-class employees and professionals. Tourism became a growth industry. Sixteen hundred kilometres of pavement in 1919 became 13 000 by 1930. Manitoba built a highway from Winnipeg to Pembina, North Dakota, as the core of its road system and only built a gravel road east to the Ontario border in 1927.

above: **By today's standards, the traffic signs in the 1920s were rudimentary. Here a policeman controls the flow of traffic with a manual Stop-and-Go sign.**

Toronto Transit Commission

below: **To hold more people, automobiles were stretched. Here a travel company takes passengers on a tour of the sights.** Vancouver Public Library, 1323

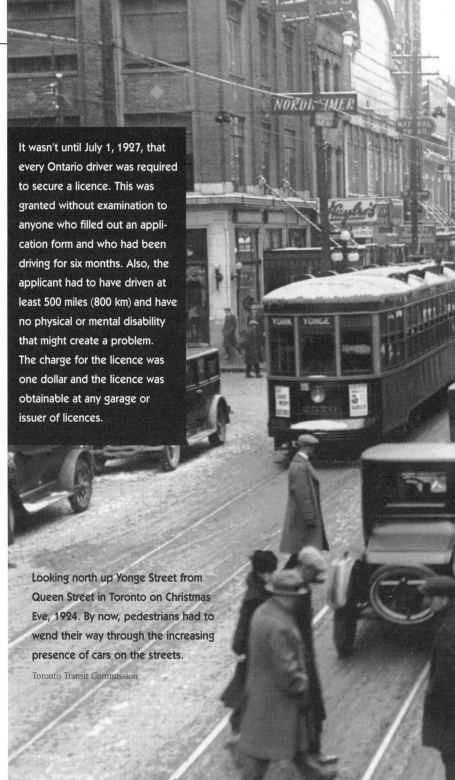

It wasn't until July 1, 1927, that every Ontario driver was required to secure a licence. This was granted without examination to anyone who filled out an application form and who had been driving for six months. Also, the applicant had to have driven at least 500 miles (800 km) and have no physical or mental disability that might create a problem. The charge for the licence was one dollar and the licence was obtainable at any garage or issuer of licences.

Looking north up Yonge Street from Queen Street in Toronto on Christmas Eve, 1924. By now, pedestrians had to wend their way through the increasing presence of cars on the streets.

Toronto Transit Commission

Patriots and the Canadian Automobile Association annually insisted on a trans-Canada Highway, but provincial governments understood where the dollars came from and built north-south instead. Americans poured north toward Vancouver, Toronto and Montreal, and when road construction permitted, pushed on to the mountains, lakes and fishing streams beyond. By the late 1920s, two to four million cars entered Canada annually from the United States. Tourist complaints forced Ontario to raise its speed limit and provide eight liquor stores on the border for thirsty Americans fleeing Prohibition. To pay for construction, provinces started taxing gasoline. Farmers and tourists were not the only people whose lives were changed by the car. More Canadians fled the winter weather for a sunnier south. Teenagers found that a car was a new place to meet, far from the family parlour and the eyes of chaperoning parents. Other lives were changed permanently. In 1928, 1006 Canadians died in car accidents, 73 of them at railway level crossings.

"Like many other inventions," the author of the Canada Year Book declared in 1930, "the motor car commenced as a toy, then became a luxury of the rich, while it now ranks as a necessity to those in moderate circumstances and it may even become a necessity of life to the masses."

That would certainly happen, but first there would be an unpleasant interruption.

above: **Mail delivery near Ottawa, 1920s.** National Archives of Canada

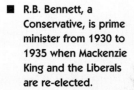

- R.B. Bennett, a Conservative, is prime minister from 1930 to 1935 when Mackenzie King and the Liberals are re-elected.

- Canadians struggle through the Great Depression. In 1932, a quarter of all workers are unemployed.

- Uranium is discovered at Great Bear Lake in 1930.

- The Co-operative Commonwealth Federation (CCF), predecessor of the New Democratic Party, is founded in 1930.

- In the West, crops fail through most of the 1930s.

- In 1934, Newfoundland goes bankrupt and reverts to being a British colony.

- The ancestor of the CBC is formed in 1934, and Trans-Canada Airlines, predecessor of Air Canada, is created in 1937.

- The Bank of Canada is created in 1935 to manage the country's monetary system.

- In 1939 Canada declares war on Germany.

Road building, such as this in Roosville, B.C., was one of a number of work projects organized by governments during the Depression. Camps were created across Canada where thousands of young men worked eight hours a day in return for food, clothing, lodging and 20 cents.

National Archives of Canada, C 20013

CHAPTER FOUR

1930-1940

TOUGH TIMES ON WHEELS

If Canada's pride in the 1920s had been a shiny new Reo or a Willys-Overland, its shame in the Depression years was the "Bennett Buggy," an aging Ford or Chev with the engine and windscreen removed, hitched to a team of plodding hay-burners.

The Depression in Canada began with failure to sell the 1928 wheat crop and headed east. Because cars were still a luxury, hard times hit the automotive industry early. Even in 1929 sales and production fell sharply as prairie farmers checked their shrinking bank balances and cancelled their orders. Factories had set their prices in hopes of mass production and lots of exports. What if no one could afford to buy? In 1930, manufacturers lost $8.04 on each car they produced. When sales were falling, how could you possibly raise prices? In 1932, the loss per car reached $103.37.

Most factories closed, throwing tens of thousands out of work. Unemployment insurance was a socialist dream. When savings vanished, people had to sell everything to qualify for welfare.

In 1930, R.B. Bennett had won the election by promising Canadians that he would raise tariffs until Canada's trading partners begged him to stop. That way, he claimed, he would "blast a way into the markets of the world." The auto industry was a good place to start: in 1931 Bennett boosted the tariff on American-made cars.

At the start of the 1930s, almost half of prairie farmers had cars. Within a couple of years, however, there was often no money for repairs or even for gas and oil. The result was the "Bennett Buggy," an automobile body stripped of its engine and drawn by a horse or even, as seen here, by an ox or two.

Glenbow Museum

left: **An out-of-work blacksmith and his family in Edmonton. They are heading back to Saskatchewan where they originally came from and hoping that their car survives to get them there.**
Saskatchewan Archives

right: **In the late 30s the Canadian Tire Corporation was franchised by its Toronto owners. By the mid 1940s there would be 71 stores in the chain.**

Into 1930, the big selling point of a car called a Superior Whippet was known as "finger tip control." Beyond tooting the horn when it was pushed, the horn button turned on the lights when it was twisted and started the engine when it was pulled up. Unfortunately, the system turned out to be failure-prone and therefore impractical.

below: **In March 24, 1931, and Ford's president (left) and the general superintendent of the plant proudly pose with the one millionth Ford car produced in Canada. It is a Model A four-door sedan.** Ford Motor Company

That was no help to car buyers or dealers. When government officials explained that tariffs kept the Ontario-based auto industry alive, C.H. O'Halloran from British Columbia reminded the Tariff Board that ordinary Canadians could not understand why the same car cost 25 percent less in Seattle than it did in a Vancouver showroom. In 1933, a Windsor customer paid $1000 for a car that cost $735 across the river in Detroit. Was an automotive industry, tucked into a corner of wealthy Ontario, a luxury Canadians could no longer afford? Would you kill an industry, demanded Ford's Wallace Campbell, that had built entire towns and cities, that had opened world markets for Canadian resources and that had created jobs for a hundred thousand people?

In some ways, Bennett's strategy worked: in October 1932, Canada gave free entry to cars built in the British Empire — provided 60 percent of the content was "Empire-made." That was good for Canada's auto parts industry. In other ways, Bennett failed. By 1934, Canada had fallen to fifth place among world auto producers. Britain, France and Germany had all moved ahead of her.

In 1936, Theodore Morgan asked the Canadian Good Roads Association for drastic measures against accidents:

The driver of a motor vehicle should be taught that he should not pass another car on a hill or curve, that he should use caution at railway crossings and highway intersections, that he should observe the white line and keep to his own side of the road at a curve, that excessive speed would not be tolerated.

The Association agreed to appoint a committee.

DANGERS OF NIGHT DRIVING

Too much speed in night driving is one trouble. If you're going 30 miles (48 km) an hour and your brakes are good, you can stop in time to avoid hitting a stationary object that you glimpse as soon as the headlights show it. Another major cause of accidents at night is that the driver is more likely to be tired. Nobody goes to sleep on a rough dirt road; the bumps take care of that. But a smooth concrete road with the steady gleam of the headlights on the pavement hypnotizing the eyes, and the purr of the motor dulling the nerves, may help to create the moment of sleep that is sufficient to let the car crash over the embankment or into an oncoming car.

Family Herald and Weekly Star, July 29, 1936

below left: **One of several Imperial oil ads done in 1934 by Group of Seven artist A. J. Casson.**

Imperial Oil Archives

left: **A 1933 ad for the new Chevrolet Six. The boxy "twenties" look and the rumble seat would soon be abandoned.**

below: **While poverty was wide-spread during the Depression, it did not affect all Canadians. Seen here in his chauffeur-driven 1930 Cadillac is John David Eaton, grandson of the T. Eaton Company founder, with his bride.**

Alexander Archives

Like other industries, automotive manufacturing slowly hauled itself out of the Depression. By 1934, companies were again making a profit. One reason was a new era of brutal labour policies. Companies cut wages and fired workers who looked likely to need the company's medical or pension plan. With one Canadian in four desperately looking for work, no one had to pretend that auto-making was a glamour-job. Instead, it became an ordeal, with arbitrary assembly-line speed-ups and massive unpaid annual layoffs when factories were retooled for the new model.

In the United States, car plants were targeted by the Congress of Industrial Organizations (CIO), a militant new union movement that organized workers whatever their craft or skill. In 1937, the CIO helped Canadians organize Sam McLaughlin's former plant at Oshawa, now owned by General Motors.

The company accepted the situation but Ontario's Liberal premier, Mitch Hepburn, did not. To frighten the workers, he organized a special police force, mainly from university students. Strikers called them "Sons of Mitches," and Oshawa's mayor insisted that there was no violence and no need for police. Hepburn's labour minister, David Croll, quit in disgust at the premier's tactics. "I would rather walk with the workers," he said, "than ride with General Motors." Still, Hepburn's pressure worked. Oshawa's auto workers kept their union but they had to pretend that they had no association with the CIO. The union held its ground and the United Autoworkers were established in Canada.

above: **Garage about 1930 and its truck that went out to provide Ontario Motor League emergency service. "Clear vision" gas pumps allowed motorists to see that they were buying clean gasoline.** Ontario Motor League

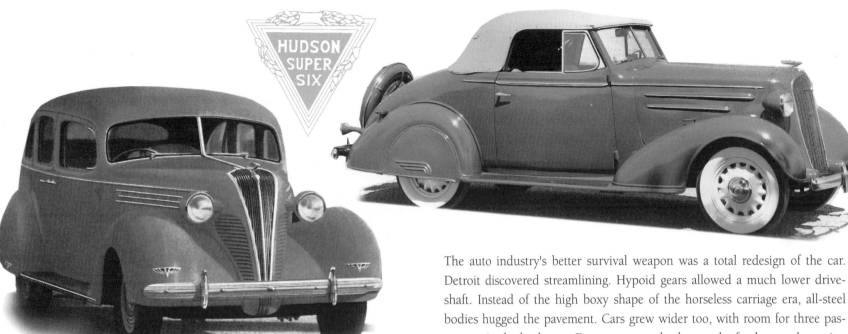

The auto industry's better survival weapon was a total redesign of the car. Detroit discovered streamlining. Hypoid gears allowed a much lower driveshaft. Instead of the high boxy shape of the horseless carriage era, all-steel bodies hugged the pavement. Cars grew wider too, with room for three passengers in the back seat. Doors were cut back over the fenders, and running boards, familiar in old-fashioned car-chase sequences, began to disappear. British cars made a bid for the Canadian market, but the harsh winters and aggressive North American marketing proved too much for them.

In January 1936, Charles N. Pogue of Winnipeg announced that he had invented a carburetor that would make it possible for a car to go 200 miles (320 km) on one gallon (4.5 L) of gasoline. Later that same year, before the device had gone into production, Pogue announced that all his working models had been stolen while he was at lunch. The thieves were never caught, the Pogue carburetor never did go into production, and rumour had it that the inventor had been "bought off" by the big oil companies.

top right: **1936 Chevrolet convertible.**

above: **The 1937 Hudson introduced a gear shift mounted to the steering column. Hudsons were made in Canada from 1932 to 1957.**

right **1939 Pontiac.**
Pontiac Division, GMC.

New cars had to cope with old roads and some new ones. Road-building was one way to put masses of unemployed men to work. By 1937, Canada boasted over 160 000 kilometres of surfaced roads, double the length only ten years earlier. In 1936, Saskatchewan had the least money and the most roads of any province in Canada: 342 516 kilometres, but only 250 of them were paved. Most of the rest were dirt trails that vanished under spring rains, winter snow and summer dust. Ontario, in contrast, had paved almost 10 000 of its 117 000 kilometres of "King's Highway" and gravelled another 78 300. British Columbia was in between. Of 33 586 kilometres of road, about 2000 boasted various hard surfaces from concrete to "bituminous mulch."

Even with so many other problems, from mass unemployment to the distant echoes of Adolf Hitler's rise to power in Germany, Canadians in the thirties found traffic accidents a serious preoccupation. In 1930, car accidents killed 1290 people. Bad times helped cut the toll to 955 dead in 1933. Terrible roads probably limited fatalities. Saskatchewan had the lowest accident rate of any province except — sometimes — Prince Edward Island. Quebec, for some reason, was the consistent leader in traffic deaths, while British Columbia was in the middle, with 78 in 1933 and 120 in 1939.

right: **United Autoworkers' strike, Oshawa, 1937.**
Archives of Labor and Urban Affairs, Wayne University

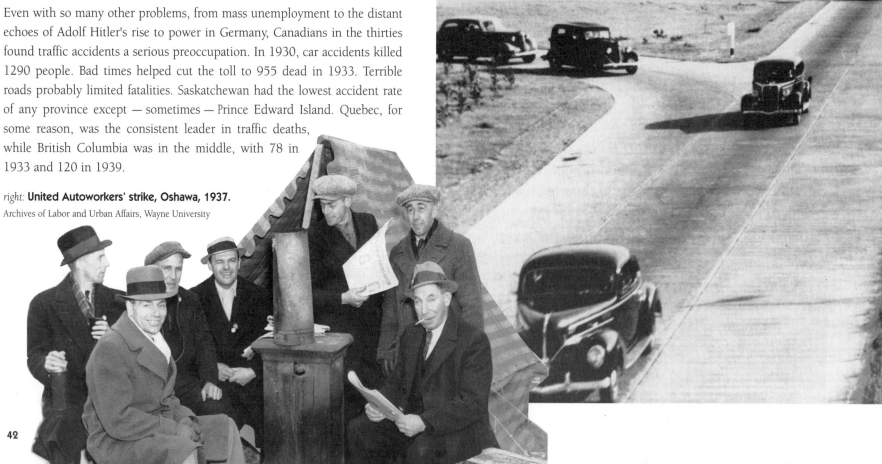

above: **September, 1939, Canada was at war with Germany. Many unemployed were the first to join up.** Toronto Telegram

left: **In 1939, The Queen Elizabeth Way ("The Queen E") opened between Hamilton and Toronto and was the first four-lane, limited-access highway in North America.** Ontario Archives

inset: **The first Royal Tour by King George VI and Queen Elizabeth in 1939. The royal cars were custom built by Chrysler.** Toronto Star

- Mackenzie King survives two elections and the war to retire as prime minister in 1948. Louis St. Laurent succeeds him.

- Canada enters the Second World War in 1939, mobilizes the greatest military and economic effort in its history and emerges as almost a major power.

- Quebec women finally win the right to vote in provincial elections in 1941.

- In 1942, Japanese Canadians are rounded up in British Columbia and sent to internment camps in the interior of the province and Ontario.

- Family allowances, unemployment insurance, veterans' benefits and other social programs mark Canada's new commitment to social justice for all.

- Discovery of a Soviet spy ring in Ottawa in September 1945 opens the Cold War.

- A major oil deposit is discovered near Edmonton, Alberta, in 1947.

- In 1949, Newfoundland becomes Canada's tenth province.

Field artillery tractor towing an anti-tank gun in Italy in December 1943. It was designed in Britain and built in Canada which was by then providing most of Britain's military vehicles.

CHAPTER FIVE

1940-1950

WHEELING TO WAR AND WEALTH

In 1939, Canada was staggering out of a second round of the Great Depression and one in six workers was still looking for a job. Two years after the war began, there were more jobs than workers to fill them. The war was unexpectedly good news for the unemployed and their families; it was bad news for most drivers and it was an enormous bonanza for Canada's auto industry.

For a government determined to finance its war effort on a pay-as-you-go basis, car owners had to be wealthy enough to pay an extra share. Excise taxes — a hidden percentage of the purchase price — rose in 1940 by anywhere from 20 to 90 percent depending on the type of vehicle and its source.

When Hitler's tanks and planes shattered the allied armies in the spring of 1940 and France collapsed, the "phony war" was over. Canada was suddenly Great Britain's most powerful ally against Nazi Germany. The country's people and industry would be mobilized as they never had been in the previous war. In a war that depended on wheels, Canada's biggest manufacturing industry was in the front line.

A 1942 Mercury, the last car Ford would produce until the war was over.

Ford Motor Company

GAS RATIONING

Gasoline was critical to the war effort and was rationed for owners of passenger cars in Canada. The following is the annual gasoline ration in 1942:

Casual, non essential	1364 L
Clergyman	2000 L
Farm truck	as required
Ambulance	as required
Bus	as required
Urban salesman	3819 L
Doctor	3819 L
Welfare worker	6365 L
Rural salesman	8819 L
U. K. diplomat	8819 L

To save rubber and gas, a speed limit was imposed on drivers. A limit of 64 km/h was set on May 1, 1942, and the fine was $15 to $50 or 10 days in jail for the first offense.

RATION BOOKS

Ration books were issued with limits of gas available, depending on specified needs. A person could be fined $5000 or sentenced to five years or both for violating the regulations.

National Archives of Canada,
C 139982

By government order, no new civilian cars were produced after 1941. Rubber tires disappeared from the stores. Gasoline was tightly rationed. Doctors — who still made house calls in the 1940s — were among the few Canadians who could do all the driving they wanted. Farmers were allowed to buy coloured gasoline, to be used only in tractors or combine harvesters. A lot of Canadians had always avoided winter driving, jacking up their cars on blocks until spring. Now patriotic citizens heeded appeals to leave them there until the war ended. Others, of course, "knew a man" who could get them a pair of "almost new" tires, a handful of ration coupons or a can of actual gasoline, probably siphoned out of someone else's tank. Suddenly there was a run on lockable caps for gas tanks.

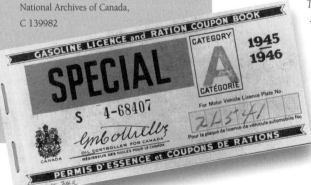

Top left: **An Imperial Oil truck driver and his daughter, British Columbia, 1940.**
Imperial Oil Archives

Top right: **In early 1942, the federal government gave in to pressure from British Columbia, rounded up the province's Japanese-Canadian population and deported them all to internment camps. Their property, including the cars seen here as well as their homes and fishing boats, was confiscated and sold at fire-sale prices.**

Vancouver Public Library, No. 1369

Military contracts gave automotive manufacturers all the business they could handle. When Britain ran out of money to pay for its purchases, the American president, Franklin Roosevelt, agreed to a Lend Lease program that he extended to Canada's production. Sure that they would be paid, businesses expanded. Top executives from the industry, including General Motors' Harry Carmichael and Ford's Wallace Campbell, became "dollar-a-year" men in Ottawa, helping to run Canada's war effort. When the United States entered the war in 1941, American-owned plants in Canada were told to go on producing British-designed "Standard Military Pattern" (SMP) vehicles as part of Washington's "Lend-Lease" assistance to the hard-pressed British.

left: **Canadian Regiments in Italy in 1943.** National Archives

below: **Canadian Division moves into France in 1944.** National Archives

Canadian factories turned out half the vehicles that carried Britain's Eighth Army across North Africa. By 1944, the 500 000th military vehicle rolled down a Canadian assembly line. It was a battery-charging truck that, tactfully, included parts from all the Big Three manufacturers. Motor vehicle manufacturing was even more important for the Allied war effort than Canada's artillery ammunition production had been in the earlier war. The relative sophistication of the two products was a measure of Canada's industrial progress between the wars.

Overseas, Canadians learned to use their mechanized tools of war to win victories. Canadian armoured divisions smashed through heavily defended enemy positions in Italy and Normandy. A Canadian general, Guy Simonds, converted some Canadian-built tanks into the first tracked armoured personnel carriers. The troops called them "kangaroos" and they saved a lot of lives.

The Germans hoped to stop the Allied armies by wrecking ports and shutting off supplies. Around the clock, long convoys of Canadian-built 3-ton trucks drove along narrow French and Belgian roads to deliver food, ammunition and fuel to the British, Canadian and American armies. Reliable trucks helped win the war in Northwest Europe.

Manufacturing techniques developed by the automobile industry were applied to building other wartime weapons, from naval guns and army machine guns to the plywood fuselages for sleek Mosquito bombers. During the war, auto industry employment doubled, investment grew by 142 percent and wages rose by 222 percent. By 1945, Ford and Chrysler plants in Windsor had been organized by the United Autoworkers.

left: **Workers meet difficulties building a highway to Alaska, circa 1943**
Yukon Archives

right: **Calling for drivers, 1944. Women were not offered this opportunity again until the 70s.** Ontario Archives

left: **In 1941 Armand Bombardier, creator of the snowmobile, was asked to build a track vehicle, but it proved unsuccessful. He took the design, put the sprockets on the front and added a pair of skis for steering. The army commissioned the building of these for troop movements and after the war it was modified and became a major commercial success.**

National Archives

Peace in 1945 brought enormous problems of readjustment. Many Canadians had looked forward to the end of the war with mixed feelings, convinced that Canada would return to the Depression conditions of the 1930s. In practice, a deliberate slowdown in output during 1944 — on the argument that the Allies already had more than enough vehicles to win the war — made it easier to return to civilian automobile production. The early postwar models looked very much like those of 1940. When Studebaker pioneered a styling breakthrough in 1947, it was — as so often with that doomed company — a little too far ahead of its time. Other once-famous car-makers like Packard and Hupmobile failed to survive the postwar adjustment. Willys-Overland, once known for big luxury cars, had become even more famous for its wartime jeeps. It joined with other companies to form American Motors, which had its Canadian headquarters in Brampton, not far from Toronto.

The chief postwar adjustment for most company management was getting used to labour unions. At Windsor, Ford workers insisted that their company "check off" union dues from their pay cheques and pay them directly to the union. That was a major issue in a 1945 strike that featured an unexpected application of the automotive age. After two months of striking and threats to use police to break their picket line, workers drove down the street in front of the factory, stopped, locked their cars and walked home. The blockade focused attention on the strike, particularly after a truckload of meat that was caught in it began to go bad. Still, it took another month to persuade Ford to accept binding arbitration.

Called in as an arbitrator, Mr. Justice Ivan Rand scolded the union for its car blockade, but he also settled the check-off issue in its favour. Workers could refuse to join a union, but they still had to pay dues for the union's work in representing them in collective bargaining and grievances. With the "Rand Formula," the auto industry gave Canada a sensible compromise between the union demand for a "closed shop" in which every worker had to belong to it and the employer's preference for leaving the cost and responsibility of unionism to a few lonely volunteers.

Union bargaining meant higher wages for millions of Canadians inside and outside unions. In turn, that helped most of them to join the ranks of car owners. In 1945, 1 497 000 automobiles were registered across Canada. By 1950, there were 2 600 000. Sprawling new suburbs, hurriedly built for veterans and their families, were habitable only with a car for getting to work and to shopping.

More cars and bad roads meant accidents. In 1944, with wartime speed restrictions in force, only 1372 Canadians had died in road accidents, far fewer than in 1940. Postwar speed limits across Canada were usually 50 miles (80 km) per hour in the country, 25 or 30 miles (40-50 km) in towns. By 1949, the annual toll was 2230 and rising.

above: **A major crude-oil discovery near Leduc, Alberta in February, 1947 changed the face of the Canadian petroleum industry.** Imperial Oil Archives

bottom: **1947 Studebaker**

Governments had to become serious about auto insurance coverage since being run down by an uninsured driver could bring financial ruin as well as physical injury. As early as 1932, British Columbia had moved to suspend drivers who could not pay court judgements; in 1947 it gave itself the power to impound the car as well. Saskatchewan's new Co-operative Commonwealth Federation (CCF) government, elected in 1944, recognized that most of the impoverished province's drivers had no insurance at all. Its solution was the world's first government-run auto insurance plan. Drivers paid for their coverage when they paid for their annual licence plates. Such "socialism" shocked private insurance companies, but the idea of a single, government-run car insurance system spread to Manitoba in 1969, British Columbia in 1972, and for basic coverage, to Quebec in 1978.

With the war over, governments could get back to road-building and paving. Politics determined the location. A Montreal magazine feature on Quebec's Union Nationale government showed how road-paving machinery played its role in a tight by-election race in the province's rural Beauce region. Once the outcome was clear, the machinery departed to a more grateful region. Similar stories might have been written about other provinces.

above: **Employees leave their cars to jam the streets outside the Windsor Ford plant during the 1945 strike.** Archives of Labor and Urban Affairs, Wayne State University

New suburban home in the late 1940s. Between 1945 and 1950, about 350 000 new dwellings were constructed. Almost all were in suburbs and included at the very least a driveway where the essential family car could be kept.

National Archives of Canada, PA 93950

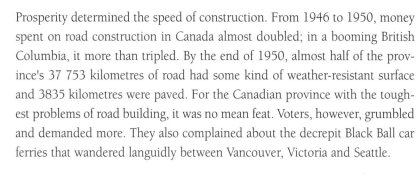

Prosperity determined the speed of construction. From 1946 to 1950, money spent on road construction in Canada almost doubled; in a booming British Columbia, it more than tripled. By the end of 1950, almost half of the province's 37 753 kilometres of road had some kind of weather-resistant surface and 3835 kilometres were paved. For the Canadian province with the toughest problems of road building, it was no mean feat. Voters, however, grumbled and demanded more. They also complained about the decrepit Black Ball car ferries that wandered languidly between Vancouver, Victoria and Seattle.

Still, roads could unite a people that, for the most part, felt prouder and more united than ever after a war. In 1946, for the first time, it was possible to drive across Canada by car without using railway tracks or logging trails. On December 10, 1949, after Newfoundland joined Canada, Ottawa promised a Trans-Canada Highway Act. Every province but Quebec agreed. The route would run from Beacon Hill on Vancouver Island to Signal Hill outside St. John's. It would be a two-lane road, 22 to 24 feet (6.7 to 7.3 m) wide and the shortest east-west route across each province. Ottawa promised to pay half the cost up to $150 million and the full cost when the route passed through national parks. Though it was officially opened in 1962, the 7725-kilometre highway was not complete until 1971 at a cost of $1.46 billion, $825 million from Ottawa.

It took 70 years, but a dream born with the automotive age finally came true.

1947 Oldsmobile

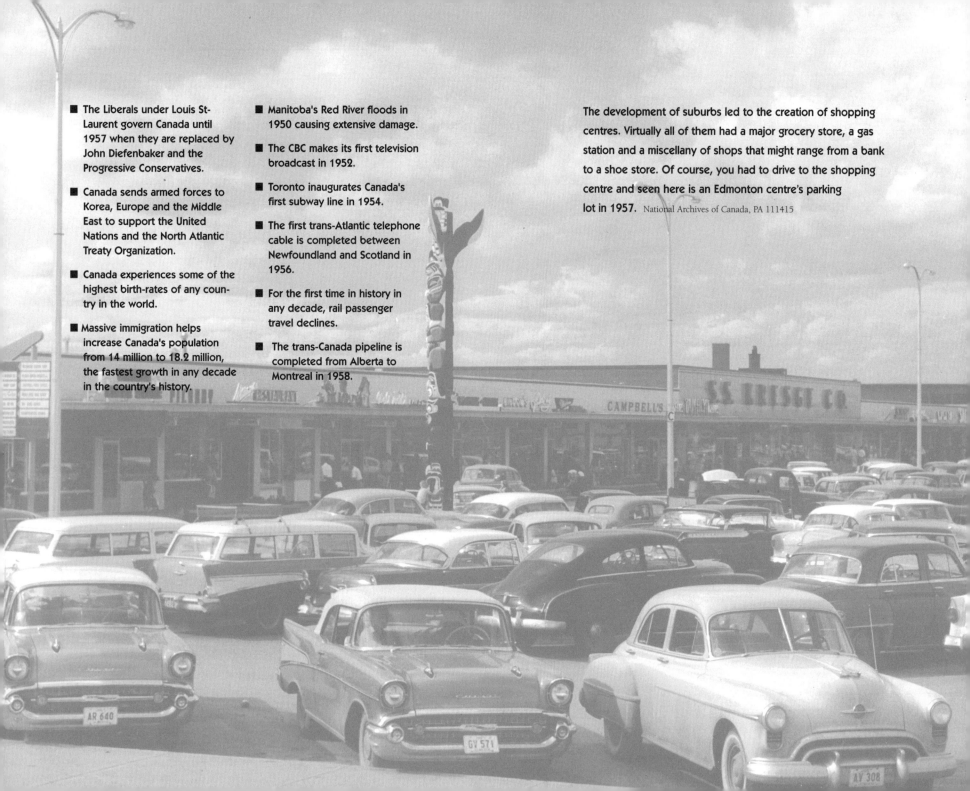

- The Liberals under Louis St-Laurent govern Canada until 1957 when they are replaced by John Diefenbaker and the Progressive Conservatives.

- Canada sends armed forces to Korea, Europe and the Middle East to support the United Nations and the North Atlantic Treaty Organization.

- Canada experiences some of the highest birth-rates of any country in the world.

- Massive immigration helps increase Canada's population from 14 million to 18.2 million, the fastest growth in any decade in the country's history.

- Manitoba's Red River floods in 1950 causing extensive damage.

- The CBC makes its first television broadcast in 1952.

- Toronto inaugurates Canada's first subway line in 1954.

- The first trans-Atlantic telephone cable is completed between Newfoundland and Scotland in 1956.

- For the first time in history in any decade, rail passenger travel declines.

- The trans-Canada pipeline is completed from Alberta to Montreal in 1958.

The development of suburbs led to the creation of shopping centres. Virtually all of them had a major grocery store, a gas station and a miscellany of shops that might range from a bank to a shoe store. Of course, you had to drive to the shopping centre and seen here is an Edmonton centre's parking lot in 1957. National Archives of Canada, PA 111415

CHAPTER SIX

1950-1960

AUTOMOTIVE AFFLUENCE

In the postwar years, Canada's highways and parking lots had looked like an automotive museum. Canadians had patched and preserved their cars through the Depression and the wartime years — undoubtedly aided by the fact that few municipalities ever used salt to melt ice or snow. Thousands of men and women had trained as drivers and mechanics during the war, and their do-it-yourself skills kept many a family's aged clunker roadworthy.

When the feared postwar depression arrived in the late 1940s, it was little more than an economic blip, soon dispelled when the United States and her allies re-armed for the Cold War with the Soviet Union. By the 1950s, the average Canadian was wealthier than most had ever dreamed of being.

The new North American cars satisfied an urge for gaudy display. Huge chrome bumpers, huge gleaming lights and audacious tail fins told the world that cars were for fun, not work. Wrap-around windows were standard. "Fluid drive" or "automatic" gear-shifting meant that the left foot had nothing better to do than beat time to the music from the car radio. The few little dials on the dashboard of prewar cars were brought together in a huge lighted display that looked like one of those miniature juke boxes in a restaurant.

1953 Ford Mercury

In the mid 1950s, there were about four million automobiles in Canada.

From the first, speed had been an irresistible attraction for car drivers — and a source of terror for other road users. Some of the airfields built for the Second World War were turned into tracks for drag racing. At Abbotsford in British Columbia, the first road race took place in 1949, and soon the auto industry was claiming that racing, with its spectacular crashes and steady toll of top drivers, was a vital part of designing safer cars.

Certainly there was a lot wrong with North American automobiles: poor cornering, soggy suspension and soaring gasoline consumption. Still, were buyers complaining? Drastic annual styling changes let the neighbours know who was driving last year's model. Rust spots and dents were another sign of last year's model, since bumpers were for show, not bumping. The real engineering innovation of the decade was "built-in obsolescence," a guarantee that customers would soon be back in the showrooms, matching wits with salesmen who had inherited their morals and some of their techniques from the notorious trade of horse-selling.

Big new cars and the rapid turn-over of used cars meant that almost everyone could finally afford a set of wheels. It was about time. Since the 1920s, cars had been redesigning the Canadian economy and the Canadian landscape. Now it was time for the cities to shape up. By the beginning of the decade, every self-respecting community had its "gasoline alleys" along the approaching highways. In addition to service stations, wreckers' yards, car dealerships and used car lots, with their characteristic coloured lights and flapping plastic banners, other businesses stationed themselves to collect the trade. The first franchised chicken and hamburger outlets began grabbing business from local "Mom 'n' Pop" diners because drivers could spot their familiar garish signs. Motels—one-storey strings of rooms in precast concrete around an asphalt parking lot—replaced the dinky little cabins that had catered to prewar motorists.

below: **Suburban development in Calgary in 1951. Row after row of similarly styled houses and not a grown tree in sight were typical of the countless number of suburbs that developed across the country in the 1950s. Garages or at least driveways were normally included as you almost certainly needed a car to get to work and shopping.** National Archives of Canada, PA 111416

The 1950s gave birth to the shopping plaza, vast parking lots bounded by rows of nationally advertised shops, usually with a grocery supermarket and a department store at either end. Downtown merchants watched sales shrink as car-borne customers headed for the outskirts. Municipal politicians were torn between schemes to help revive a dying downtown and the promise of fresh revenue from yet another plaza development. Few resisted the temptation. By the end of the decade, developers were designing the first covered malls, vast halls of commerce where customers could escape rain, snow, summer heat and winter cold. Outside, acres of cars waited for their owners.

top right: **Now that the car was a common presence, many found entertainment at the drive-in theatre, particularly those with young children. Just hook up the speaker and the heater and soon the children would be asleep and you could watch the movie on the big screen.**

bottom right: **By the mid-1950s, numerous motels were springing up along highways heading in and out of cities. This one was on Winnipeg's Pembina Highway, near the university. Its use was very astute: during the winter, when there were few tourists, it rented several of its units to car-owning, out-of-town students who wanted a little more freedom and privacy than university residences tended to provide.**

Jocelyn Smyth

Immigration to Canada ballooned after the war. Between 1946 and 1958, nearly 2 million arrived.

Trucks were challenging railways as the movers of Canada's freight by the mid-1950s. It was estimated, in fact, that approximately 10 percent of all urban freight was now moving in trucks. National Archives of Canada, PA 111418

The flat western prairies provided ideal conditions for the construction of the trans-Canada pipeline from Alberta to Montreal.

Imperial Oil Archives

At the beginning of the 1950s just over 50% of households had at least one automobile. By the end of the decade the number had risen to nearly 70%.

The population increased with the birth of "baby boomers" during the 1950s with nearly 4.5 million births. The population of Canada grew from 14 million at the beginning of the 1950s to 18 million a decade later, an increase of nearly 30%.

A huge investment in paving and gravel ended the isolation of rural life almost everywhere in Canada. It also killed many of the crossroads communities where farm people had worshiped, gone to school and done their weekly shopping. An 80-kilometre journey to town was now an hour's drive, not a day's exhausting adventure. The bright lights and the bargains made it all worthwhile.

The continuing love affair with the automobile coincided with trouble in Canada's biggest manufacturing industry. The war had killed the country's role as a major auto exporter to the Commonwealth and the world. What war-wracked country could afford to spend scarce dollars for a Canadian-made car? Major prewar buyers of Canadian cars, like Australia, Argentina and South Africa, wanted their own automobile industry, even if it depended on the same American corporations that ran Canada's factories. Now instead of exporting, Canada became a market for other auto-makers. In the 1950s, imports began to squeeze the three big auto makers who dominated Canadian parking lots: General Motors, Ford and Chrysler. Annual production from Canada's factories fell from 297 373 cars in 1955 to 274 602 in 1958. Foreign imports rose from 13 percent of Canadian production to 51.1 percent.

top: **Note the 1950s dashboard with the knobs and a steering column that does not collapse in a collision. The car itself has no windshield washing system yet either, but service is given with a smile by the gas station attendant.**

Imperial Oil Archives

bottom: **1955 BelAir convertible.**
Chevrolet Division, General Motors Ltd.

The reasons varied. As a postwar boost to British recovery, Canada had allowed English cars to enter duty-free. Few Canadians admired their quality, service or adaptability to the tough Canadian winter, but the price was right. Soon, better and even cheaper European cars appeared. German-made Volkswagens were the champions. With their distinctive beetle shape and cheeky advertising, owning a Volks became a reverse status symbol for people who found the Detroit-style dream car grotesque, expensive and inefficient. By the end of the 1950s, the future for Canadian auto plants and their workers was starting to look grim. Even if they knew how to compete, there was no way for the branch plant of an American giant to match the quality or style of the imports. Only in 1959 did American head offices approve the first "compacts" as a cautious response to European competition.

Sam McLaughlin, "Mr. Sam," builder of the McLaughlin cars, formed General Motors of Canada in 1918. He had a long and distinguished life and at the age of 98 he was still chairman of the board of General Motors of Canada. He is seen here standing between an old McLaughlin and a new 1959 General Motors car.

General Motors of Canada

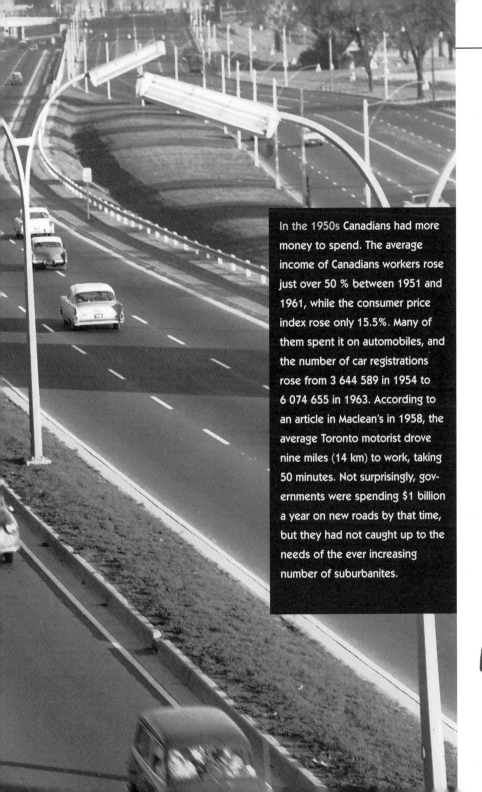

In the 1950s Canadians had more money to spend. The average income of Canadians workers rose just over 50 % between 1951 and 1961, while the consumer price index rose only 15.5%. Many of them spent it on automobiles, and the number of car registrations rose from 3 644 589 in 1954 to 6 074 655 in 1963. According to an article in Maclean's in 1958, the average Toronto motorist drove nine miles (14 km) to work, taking 50 minutes. Not surprisingly, governments were spending $1 billion a year on new roads by that time, but they had not caught up to the needs of the ever increasing number of suburbanites.

In Ottawa, the government looked for the best advice it could get from a Toronto economics professor, Vincent Bladen. His report in 1962 had lots of ideas. Imports, he argued, had an unfair advantage because of low wages and cheap shipping costs. Canada should restore the import duty on British-made cars and remove the excise tax on Canadian-made cars. Most of the jobs in the auto industry belonged in the parts plants that served the big assembly lines. To help them, Bladen suggested that cars with enough "Canadian content" be allowed to enter Canada duty-free. That would be a big incentive to American firms to buy more parts in Canada.

Bladen's report got the usual one-day treatment from newspapers, radio and television. Politicians promised to study it. Canada's auto industry sagged some more. Outside southern Ontario, not many Canadians noticed.

left: **Highways multiplied in the 1950s as people moved to the suburbs to live and to cottages to vacation.** National Archives of Canada, PA 111447

below: **In an era of large cars with garish fins, some people wanted a simpler, more economical car to drive and found it in the Volkswagen "Beetle." You could travel farther for less and it was reliable, even if heating in winter was a constant problem. The Beetle was so popular that sales in Canada grew from just 52 units in 1952, when they were first imported and sold in Canada, to some 25 000 a year by the end of the decade.**

The Beetle's heyday continued into the 1970s but sales ended in Canada in 1979. In 1998 its reintroduction caused a buying mania. Improvements included a water-cooled engine up front and a six-speaker stereo.

- In 1963, the Liberals under Lester B. Pearson replace John Diefenbaker's Conservatives. Five years later, in 1968, Pierre Elliott Trudeau becomes Liberal leader and prime minister.

- Canada's two major airlines begin jet service in 1961.

- Saskatchewan doctors go on strike in 1962 when the province introduces the country's first medicare program.

- In 1964, Parliament adopts Canada's maple leaf flag.

- In 1964, Canadian troops are sent to Cyprus as part of a United Nations peace-keeping force.

- The Canada Pension Plan is introduced and Montreal hosts Canada's centennial celebration with Expo 67.

- The rest of Canada becomes aware of Quebec's "Quiet Revolution" and "separatism."

- In 1969, the Trudeau government wins all-party approval of the Official Languages Act.

- The "Big Generation" of baby-boomers revolution-izes a staid, rather boring Canada with their clothes, music and fresh ideas.

As Vancouver boomed in the 1960s, suburbs grew and expressways arrived to bear commuters to the city centre.

National Archives of Canada, PA 111266

CHAPTER SEVEN

1960-1970

SAVING AN INDUSTRY

When the rest of the Canadian economy began pulling out of the late-1950s slump, the car industry was the big exception. Whether the cars were American, European or, all of a sudden, Japanese, more and more Canadian buyers were settling for foreign-made models. Prophets of gloom found it easy to show that, if the trend continued, Canada would have no auto industry at all by the 1980s. There was a little local comfort in the Maritimes when, in 1964, Volvo opened a small assembly plant in Dartmouth for its sturdy, Swedish-designed sedans and another company opened to assemble "Canadian" Renaults.

Vincent Bladen had given the Diefenbaker government some good old-fashioned Canadian advice: high tariffs. Make the price of a foreign car so high that Canadians would have to buy Canadian-made models and the car factories would be booming again. But if all cars became more expensive, how many people could afford them? More important, how many could afford a new model every two or three years?

The Liberal Party had a different idea: create incentives that would persuade Canadian-based factories to undertake the costly business of exporting to the world. If production expanded, so would jobs, while the cost of producing each car would go down. The incentives looked so good to the Studebaker people that they closed their American factory and moved to Hamilton. Unfortunately, the strain killed the historic old firm and it did not seem to help anyone else. Somebody — and lots of people claim the credit — had a better idea. Why not create a special kind of free-trade deal only for car makers?

Ford's sporty, low-priced Mustang was a successful car throughout the decade.

By the mid-1960s there was a passenger car for every four Canadians and a vehicle for every three persons in Canada. In all, there was a total registration of 6 million vehicles and almost 7 million drivers. Registration fees and fuel taxes amounted to more than $800 million.

Cars and parts could cross the border duty-free, but only if they were sent straight to manufacturers. The Big Three automakers, General Motors, Ford and Chrysler, were delighted. A single Canada-U.S. auto market suited them fine. Wages in Canada were lower than in the United States and that would cut the costs of cars and parts made north of the border. At the same time, when the deal was signed, Canadians found that their share of total North American production had to stay at its 1964 level.

The Canada-U.S. Auto Trade Agreement of January 1965 seemed to be good news for both countries. It was certainly welcome in Ontario. Within a couple of years, the deal had helped create 19 000 well-paid new jobs. Instead of fading, the auto industry started to grow. Soon a new General Motors plant at Ste-Thérèse spread the industry to Quebec.

PUT A TIGER IN YOUR TANK!

ESSO EXTRA

1968

ALL-OUT QUALITY ESSO EXTRA GASOLINE BOOSTS POWER THREE

1 Cleaning Power! Deposits can clog ... buretor in a few months

2 Firing Power! Spark plug and cylinder deposits can cause misfiring, pre-ignition and hot spots. Esso Extra neutralizes these ... ... to help your engine fire ...

3 Octane Power! Esso high octane that high-c... now need for full smoo... without knocking. You ... extras with all-out qua...

None of this helped a Canadian to understand why a car built in Oshawa or Windsor cost a lot less in a Buffalo or Seattle showroom than it did in Hamilton or Burnaby. Still, by the 1970s, 60 000 Canadians had jobs in the auto industry and another 65 000 worked for Canadian car dealers.

Customers seemed to be a higher priority for dealers than for car-makers in the 1960s. Americans and Canadians had welcomed the affluent 1950s by having bigger families. A "baby boom" had over-crowded maternity wards and schools; by the 1960s, it was surging into universities and colleges with a buying power no generation had ever known. The auto industry met the Big Generation with "muscle cars," over-sized, over-priced versions of the neat little sports cars children of the wealthy had imported from England and Germany in the 1950s. Ford's 1964 Mustang became a classic — but it and its competitors soon showed their rust spots.

far left: **The '68 GTO was Pontiac's classic "Muscle Car"—a big car with a huge engine.** Pontiac Division, General Motors Ltd

left: **Dreamed up in the early 1960s, "Put a tiger in your tank" is still considered Imperial Oil's greatest fuel promotion slogan of all time.** Imperial Oil Archives

Canadian auto racing finally came of age at Mosport near Bowmanville, Ontario, on June 24, 1961. British racing driver Stirling Moss beat an international field on the new 4-kilometre course. Soon there were rival tracks at Edmonton and St-Jovite. The first Canadian-American, or Can-AM, challenge for sports cars was held in 1966. On August 27, 1967, to celebrate Canada's centennial, Mosport hosted the first Canadian Grand Prix for Formula One. In 1978, when the race moved to Montreal, the winner was Gilles Villeneuve. Canada's most successful racing driver, Villeneuve won six world championships before he died in a crash in 1982. Years later, his son, Jacques Villeneuve, would become a world-class Formula One driver.

CANADIAN-U.S. AUTOMOBILE TRADE AGREEMENT

Agreement was reached in 1965 by which the U.S. undertook to remove its tariff on vehicles and parts for original equipment from Canada. For its part, Canada agreed to provide conditional free entry of the same goods from the U.S. Conditions were placed on the Canadian vehicle producers: (1) Must continue to produce motor vehicles in Canada in the same ratio to sales as in the 1964 model year; (2) continue to maintain Canadian content in Canadian vehicle production; (3) increase production by the percentage of normal economic growth; (4) increase production in Canada by specific mounts, about one-third annually, by 1968.

Passenger car production increased from 323 638 units in 1961 to 687 547 in 1966 to 1 094 208 in 1971— a gigantic increase in only a decade.

above: **Autoworkers.** General Motors of Canada

The "Big Generation" wanted a good time; it also had ideals. Some people called it the "liberation" generation, and one target for liberation was North America's car culture. A dark, intense young American lawyer named Ralph Nader became an overnight hero when he took on General Motors single-handed and won. GM's Corvair, a rear-engine compact, was "unsafe at any speed," reported Nader, and his evidence came from the company's own tests. The huge corporation finally wilted.

If the Corvair could be positively dangerous, few cars were very safe. On both sides of the border in the 1960s, critics demanded pollution controls, bumpers that could absorb a bump, and car interiors that did not impale passengers in a crash. California finally admitted that its chronic smog was thickened daily by emissions from ten million car exhausts, and voters demanded a clean-up. Emission controls became a standard feature by the end of the decade. Unleaded fuels were finally available at the gas pumps. Of course the controls increased gas consumption, but who cared at less than five cents a litre?

below: **The Chevrolet Corvair was attractive and popular. However, Ralph Nader** (*above*) **in the US and others found it "unsafe at any speed," leading to its fall from popularity. It soon was taken off the market.**

above **Small European cars had started coming to Canada in the 1950s and their sales grew steadily in the 1960s.**

Smog caused by emissions from car exhausts was already a problem in downtown Toronto in the late 60s.

The car became the barometer of the economy and social attitudes. In Canada at the beginning of the 1960s, Ford sold only six models of their cars, and most of these were directed to low and middle income customers. By the end of the decade, Ford customers had a choice of twenty-three models, and a third of these could be called luxury cars.

In 1968 motor vehicle traffic accidents reported in Canada numbered 484 436.

The first car made in Canada under the Studebaker nameplate appeared in 1913 and Canadian production continued until 1936, then stopped and it wasn't until after the Second World War that Studebaker acquired a plant in Hamilton and resumed production. Finally, in March 1966, production of Studebakers ceased and were no longer made either in Canada or the United States.

top: **1915 Studebaker made in Walkerville, Ontario**

centre: **1947 Studebaker**

bottom: **1962 Studebaker Gran Turismo Hawk** Oldsmobile Division, GMC

TRANS-CANADA HIGHWAY 1964
Ministry of Transport and Communications

**FATHER OF THE
TRANS-CANADA HIGHWAY**

Dr. Perry Doolittle is known as "Father of the Trans-Canada Highway" because of his enthusiastic support for a highway that united all of Canada. Although there was no trans-Canada highway in 1925, Doolittle and Ed Flickenger drove across the country in a Ford Model T, beginning on September 8 from Halifax. After the grueling excursion, they finally reached Vancouver on October 17. During the 1930s and 1940s provinces built trunk highways. In 1946 the first trip on an all-Canadian road was completed in only nine days. Dr. Doolittle died in 1933 and did not live to see his highway completed, but he is remembered for his dedication.

Downtown Brandon, Manitoba, 1961
National Archives of Canada, PA 111388

The Trans-Canada Highway formally opened on July 30, 1962, making it possible to drive all the way from Victoria to St. John's, Newfoundland. Some 3000 kilometres remained unpaved, however, and the highway wasn't actually finished until 1970. By then, the total cost had reached $1 billion and the Trans-Canada was the longest highway in the world.

In the early 1960s, New Brunswick had 14 000 miles (32 530 km) of road, with 3000 (4830 km) of it paved and 145 000 registered vehicles, 75 percent of which were passenger cars.

During the 1950s, the United States government had poured billions into interstate freeways, all in the name of national defence. When Canadians travelled south, they came home with an appetite for more and better roads. Provincial treasurers had to squeeze out money to build multi-laned highways. Ontario had slowly pushed Highway 400 as far north as Barrie; in the 1960s, it linked Windsor and the Quebec border on a brand new Highway 401, pushed freeways through several of its bigger cities and made big plans for more. Montreal in the 1960s still lacked a municipal sewage treatment plant, but it found billions to crisscross the city with super highways in time for Expo 67 and used the dirt from an impressive new subway system to build the Expo site on islands in the St. Lawrence River. In 1967, Canada had over 400 000 kilometres of paved road in a total federal-provincial-municipal network of 1 421 000 kilometres.

Some citizens noted an odd phenomenon: the traffic jams seemed to keep pace with the new highways, just as if roads themselves attracted cars. And, of course, they did. Some of those people began to wonder whether highways and cars were a solution or a great big problem. The automobile age was rolling into a crisis.

The 1964 Plymouth Fury, started as a popular General Motors model, but times were changing and it disappeared with the decade.

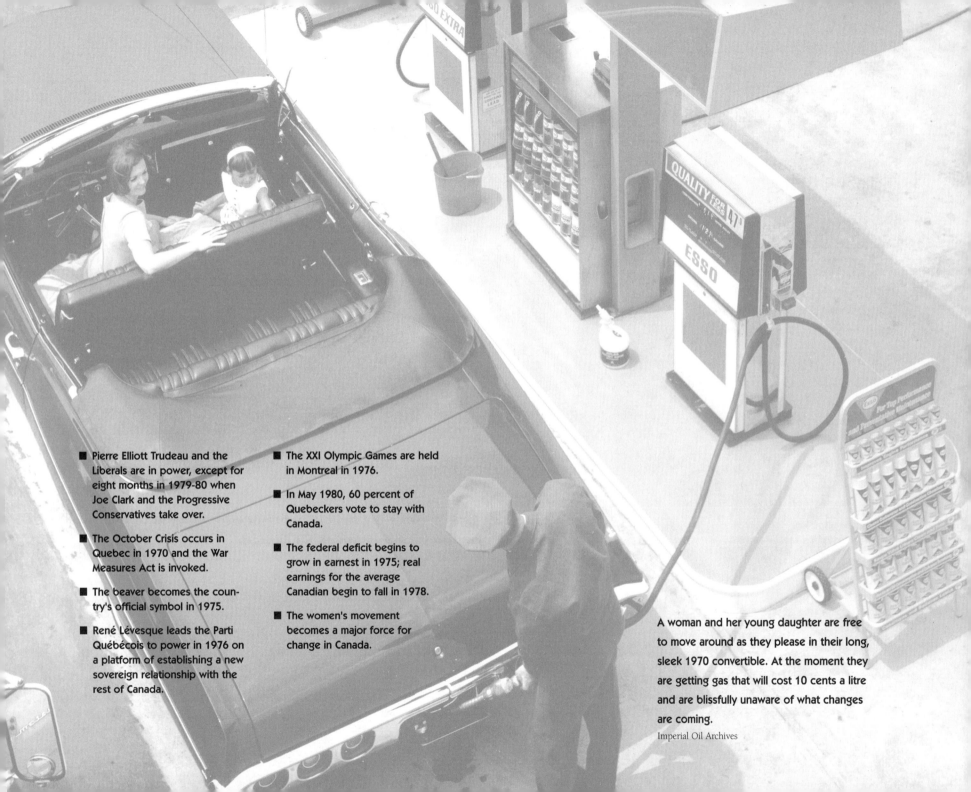

- Pierre Elliott Trudeau and the Liberals are in power, except for eight months in 1979-80 when Joe Clark and the Progressive Conservatives take over.

- The October Crisis occurs in Quebec in 1970 and the War Measures Act is invoked.

- The beaver becomes the country's official symbol in 1975.

- René Lévesque leads the Parti Québécois to power in 1976 on a platform of establishing a new sovereign relationship with the rest of Canada.

- The XXI Olympic Games are held in Montreal in 1976.

- In May 1980, 60 percent of Quebeckers vote to stay with Canada.

- The federal deficit begins to grow in earnest in 1975; real earnings for the average Canadian begin to fall in 1978.

- The women's movement becomes a major force for change in Canada.

A woman and her young daughter are free to move around as they please in their long, sleek 1970 convertible. At the moment they are getting gas that will cost 10 cents a litre and are blissfully unaware of what changes are coming.

Imperial Oil Archives

CHAPTER EIGHT

1970-1980

CARS, GAS AND THE ENVIRONMENT

The love affair with the big, fat North American automobile ended in the seventies. Canadians stopped sneering at neighbours who bought tiny German or Japanese cars and turned envious. For the "liberation generation," critical of much that their parents had admired, the big auto makers were an easy target. Demands that governments force manufacturers to deliver quality, safety and environmental protection instead of chrome and dreams rose to a volume politicians could not ignore.

The movement was continental. The catalytic converter, perfected in 1971, cut exhaust pollution dramatically, though manufacturers insisted that few car buyers wanted it. However, when California demanded emission controls in an effort to reduce its notorious smog, other American states and Canadian provinces followed suit. In 1971, Ottawa passed a Motor Vehicle Safety Act, setting standards that the American government was

already enforcing. Seat belts became a standard safety feature in cars and most provinces soon began enforcing their use. An early casualty of the safety movement was the convertible, a car with a canvas or vinyl roof that could be folded back. "Rag-tops," as the industry called them, became rare, treasured souvenirs.

1972 Oldsmobile
General Motors

JAPANESE CARS

The phenomenal growth of the Japanese auto industry started in the 1960s. From 70 000 units produced in 1955, it jumped over the million mark for 1963 and was producing five times that many by 1970. In 1978, the country exported more than 4.6 million vehicles with the United States as its largest market.

1974 Datsun

In the early 1970s, North America's car makers finally broke down and started producing smaller cars in order to try and win back the sales that were going to Europe and Japan. Seen here is American Motors' 1972 Gremlin.

American Motors

Some governments cut their highway-building plans and began channeling more money into public transit. Governments that planned expressways across cities could now count on a passionate and successful protest from residents. In 1971, the Ontario government forgot about the two billion dollars it had already lavished on developing the Spadina Expressway into the heart of Toronto. Its new devotion to downtown neighbourhoods helped win it easy re-election. Other politicians took their cue. Across Canada, transit systems were in fashion; urban expressways were not.

Nothing led to fresh thinking as much as the oil price shock in 1973. Gasoline had always seemed the cheapest part of owning a car. Suddenly, in the spring of that year, drivers learned of OPEC — the Arab-dominated Organization of Petroleum Exporting Countries — when its members forced up the world price of crude oil. In the autumn, when Arab states launched a war on Israel, OPEC reduced its exports and sent prices soaring again. When oil companies passed on the increase, prices at gasoline pumps doubled. They also rose for everything made from petroleum derivatives, from tires to plastic ornaments. As stocks dwindled, governments dusted off old wartime schemes for gas rationing.

In 1979, there was another oil price shock when Iranians overthrew the Shah, set up an Islamic republic and challenged the world by persuading its OPEC partners to curb exports once again and force up prices. To reduce gas consumption, governments across the United States and Canada cut the speed limit. Ingenious regulations were devised to prod manufacturers into building smaller, more fuel-efficient vehicles. However, when Joe Clark's new government proposed to raise gasoline prices to pay part of the huge cost of subsidizing provinces dependent on OPEC-priced oil, Canadian voters switched to the Liberals.

right: **Special seats for babies started being sold and seat belts for everybody else installed in the 1970s. It would take a while, but eventually use of them would become mandatory across the country.** Ontario Ministry of Transportation

below right: **In the 1960s and 1970s larger and larger numbers of Torontonians were opposing construction of the Spadina Expressway through some of the city's highly residential areas. In the summer of 1971, they won and the expressway from Highway 401 stopped dead well north of its lakeshore destination.** Globe and Mail

below: **1972 Ford Pinto**

THINK PEOPLE ¡STOP! SPADINA

Not everyone got their timing right. Inspired by a fast-talking Florida promoter named Malcolm Bricklin, New Brunswick premier Richard Hatfield decided to give his province a share of the auto industry. With its fibreglass body and doors that opened outward like gull wings, the Bricklin certainly looked great, and the price, $2200, when it was put on show in New York in 1974, was reasonable. The trouble was that the car didn't work very well and the actual cost of the 2880 cars ultimately produced was $13 000 each — almost all of it paid by taxpayers. Bricklin departed, New Brunswickers proved forgiving, and Hatfield survived as premier for two more terms.

Earlier, the Diefenbaker government had protected a high-cost domestic oil industry in western Canada by compelling Ontario and British Columbia to "Buy Canadian." By 1974, Canadian oil looked cheap. Instead of cashing in on the oil price bonanza by exporting to the United States, Alberta was forced to sell its oil more cheaply to Ontario and Quebec. Canadian taxpayers helped subsidize the price of imported oil in the Maritimes. The government also encouraged companies to hunt for new reserves of oil and natural gas. This might have been seen as a marvellous example of how Confederation worked in a crisis. Instead, consumers complained that they were paying too much, while Alberta and Saskatchewan insisted that they had been robbed of the right to get the best possible price for a dwindling natural resource. The fight over oil prices turned into a bitter feud between producing and consuming provinces. In Calgary, a bumper sticker declared: "Let the Eastern Bastards Freeze in the Dark."

Meanwhile, prophets of gloom predicted that cars would be obsolete in a decade when the world ran out of petroleum. Millions of dollars, mostly from the taxpayers, poured into research on electric-powered cars and on fuels that ranged from wood alcohol to pig manure. For all the fuss, remarkably little changed. In the decade that supposedly spelled doom for the car, Canada's number of motor vehicles rose steadily. By 1980, car registration reached twelve million — almost one for every two Canadian men, women and children. "Keep on truckin'" was a slogan of the time, and most Canadians did. One reason was a practical application of the "women's liberation" movement: more and more women went to work and lived their own lives. A second car in a family was no mere convenience.

opposite page: **At 10:12 AM on April 21, 1976, the last convertible came off Cadillac's assembly line in Detroit. Other convertible makes had been given up earlier, and some would come back a dozen or so years later, but they wouldn't reach the popularity they had in the 1950s and 1960s.** General Motors

above left: **The 1970s saw more and more Canadians heading off on their holidays in trailers or with campers to spend holidays at a Lake of the Woods campsite or see the western mountains or any number of other wondrous sights.** Chrysler Canada

LET THE EASTERN BASTARDS FREEZE IN THE DARK !

SAM McLAUGHLIN

Sam McLaughlin was born in Enniskillen, Ontario on September 8, 1871 and died on January 6. 1972. In that span of a hundred years, he was a pioneer in Canadian and, in fact, world development of the automobile.

In 1867, his father began making passenger sleighs and founded the McLaughlin Carriage Company. Ten years later the company moved to Oshawa, Ontario, and in 1907 it began production of motor cars under the name of McLaughlin Motor Company. The first McLaughlin car was a Model F, a two-cylinder, 22 horsepower touring car that cost the lucky buyer only $1400 but had no top or windshield. In 1918, just before it was sold to General Motors, the company was producing 125 cars a week that were known for their luxury and distinctiveness. "Mr. Sam", as he was known, became president of General Motors of Canada. He served as president until 1945, and as chairman of the board until his death.

Under Sam McLaughlin's direction, GM of Canada products had a distinctive Canadian flavour. In 1933 the Canadian Chevrolet had dozens of special touches, including a single key for all the locks. "It's better because it's Canadian" was a favourite slogan. The first new GM Canada car to go into production was the 1921 Oldsmobile, and during the 1920s the company expanded with plants in Walkerville and Regina. During that decade and the next, the flagship car was the McLaughlin-Buick.

Mr Sam's interests outside business included art collecting and horse racing. He was a major benefactor to universities and hospitals across the country. At the age of 98, he was still chairman of the board and came to his office every morning. He had built the company into a major Canadian manufacturer.

Still, the jump in oil prices and the prospect of scarcity to come had its impact. City cores became more attractive to wealthier Canadians who could afford to renovate run-down neighbourhoods and move closer to their jobs in downtown office blocks. People whose cars had carried them out to the suburbs now began to move back, leaving the increasingly slow and dreary business of commuting to others. Suburbs and smaller communities fought back by planning their own city cores. The big investment in buses, subways and commuter trains stopped the steady decline in transit riders, though rising fares helped keep many commuters in their cars.

On both sides of the border, drastic changes in legislation and economics wrought havoc with the auto industry and its suppliers. Smaller, lighter cars, designed to meet American fuel efficiency regulations, required less steel — a blow to the auto industry's biggest industrial partner. Scrambling to imitate the foreign cars that most buyers now preferred left the North American producers coming up second-best despite billions of dollars of investment. Canada's share of the industry suffered. After 1971, Canada imported far more cars and parts than it exported. Without the 1965 Auto Trade Pact, matters would probably have been even worse, but that was small comfort to the men and women who lost their jobs and the communities that had to support them.

By the end of the 1970s, most Canadians were driving the safest, most efficient and dependable cars ever produced for the mass market, but the Canadian factories that helped produce them were still in trouble.

Pontiac's 1979 Firebrand Trans-Am Coupe, produced for the tenth Firebird anniversary.

Pontiac Motor Division, General Motors

AUTOPACT

The Canada-US Automotive Products Agreement, commonly known as the "Autopact", was a trade agreement made in 1965 between the countries. Through this agreement the auto industries of Canada and the US were intended to be integrated in. Canada benefited from larger and more specialized production runs and provided safeguards to the industry. This was done by guaranteeing that if the auto companies wanted to sell in the Canadian market, they also had to reach certain levels of production in Canada. Companies that produced 50 percent or more of their vehicles in Canada and the United States could ship vehicles and components without duty across the border.

above: Workers on the assembly line. By the end of the century, many jobs on the assembly line were replaced by robotic technology. Labour Gazette

- In 1984, Brian Mulroney and the Progressive Conservatives win power from the Liberals under John Turner.

- "O Canada" is officially proclaimed the national anthem in 1980.

- Quebeckers reject sovereignty-association in 1980, but in 1990 other Canadians reject the Meech Lake Accord embodying Quebec's constitutional conditions.

- Canada's Constitution Act, with an amending formula and a Charter of Rights and Freedoms, becomes law in 1982.

- In 1984, Jeanne Sauvé becomes the first woman to be installed as Governor General of Canada.

- Canadian chemist John Polanyi receives the Nobel Prize for chemistry in 1986.

- The Canada-U.S. Free Trade Agreement is signed in 1989 after Canadians re-elect Brian Mulroney.

After cars have served their time, the next stage is in the graveyard of cars. They will be compressed and recycled for many different uses.
Ken Pearson

CHAPTER NINE

1980-1990

LUCK AND BAD MANAGEMENT

Canada's postwar prosperity was interrupted by a series of recessions — in 1949, 1959, 1971 and again in 1982 and 1990. Economic growth went into reverse, people stopped buying, factories and stores closed, and unemployment grew. Those with long memories said this was not as bad as the old "depression" when there was no unemployment insurance and "relief" was provided only when people had lost everything, including their pride. However, for people affected, modern recessions were bad enough.

Since a new car was not something you bought if times looked tough, sales plummeted. Production followed. In Canada, ten thousand jobs in the auto parts industry vanished, and seven thousand on the assembly lines.

The Big Three auto makers, some of the biggest corporations in the world, were in trouble. After losing $1 billion in 1979 and $1.7 billion in 1980 — a record loss for any business at the time — Chrysler might have gone bankrupt except for help from Washington and Ottawa. So desperate was the company to get its workers to cut their wages that it elected Doug Fraser, American head of the United Auto Workers, to the Chrysler board. His union members began to give away hard-won benefits to keep their jobs.

The economic power of women as consumers began to grow as more and more moved into higher income occupations. Targeting women as consumers, particularly car purchasers, became the wave of marketing and by the late 1980s women were buying 45% of cars and influencing 80% of all car-buying decisions.

But not in Canada. In 1982, with the auto industry seemingly in deep trouble, the UAW's Canadian leader, Bob White, ignored economists and editors and insisted on improved pay and conditions for his members. When a horrified UAW refused to back him, White led his members into a new Canadian Autoworkers Union (CAW). Was he crazy? Or were the experts not as expert as White? After the two oil price shocks of the 1970s, fuel prices stopped climbing and even fell. Americans resumed their love affair with big cars. The auto makers based in the United States had kept production of new compacts and small cars there, leaving big car production to their Canadian subsidiaries. But big cars were what buyers in the 1980s now wanted. When Canadian auto workers went on strike, dealers got the companies back to bargaining. Besides, as White pointed out, with Medicare and other tax-paid benefits, Canadian labour costs were still cheaper than American. The new Canadian union got off to a victorious start. White began spreading his organization to other workers, from fish packers to airline clerks.

above: **Auto worker Bob White plans bargaining strategy in negotiations with General Motors.** United Auto Workers

bottom: **Japanese cars— Mazda and Toyotas, 1988**

In 1982, Canada's auto exports to the United States exceeded imports from there for the first time since 1971. American politicians cried foul. However, Canadians and Americans agreed on another trading villain: the Japanese. During the recession, people kept on buying imports. Why not? They were usually cheaper, better quality and more reliable. But what about Canadian jobs? In 1981, Ottawa persuaded the Japanese to limit the number of cars they sent to Canada to 18 percent of the market. A year later, when the Japanese did not want to renew the deal, Ottawa ordered customs officers at Vancouver to take their time inspecting imported Japanese cars. Soon there was a huge backlog — and threats from Tokyo to retaliate against Canadian coal and lumber.

Economic recovery eased the pain. To most people's surprise, the recession ended and 1984 turned into a boom year for Canada and the auto industry. Sales rose 32 percent and auto-product exports climbed by 26.8 percent. Japanese auto companies made peace with Washington and Ottawa by building assembly plants in the United States and Canada. Soon Honda had a new factory at Alliston and CAMI, a partnership of General Motors and Suzuki, was building cars near Woodstock. A Korean manufacturer, Hyundai, accepted $115 million in bonuses and tax concessions to open a factory at Bromont in Quebec. The export restrictions persuaded the Japanese to ship bigger, higher-quality cars to North America, and their share of the automobile market kept on growing. The Big Three invested too. The $3.7 billion Autoplex at Oshawa was the continent's biggest auto assembly plant, with up-to-date computers and robots to build the new Lumina. Ford spent $1 billion at Oakville and $59 million to cast aluminum engine blocks at Windsor.

By the mid-1980s there were 11 million passenger cars, one for every 2.3 persons. In the late 1980s, Canadians bought about one million new cars, trucks and vans per year for private use. The total amount spent including purchase price, parts, repairs and operation, accounted for almost 12% of all personal spending.

The car industry led the way in "going global." Instead of making all or most of their cars and trucks, companies "out-sourced" to parts manufacturers all over the world. Computers helped suppliers to get their parts delivered "just in time" so manufacturers did not have to store a big inventory of items. Factories in China, Malaya and Mexico produced bumpers, headlights, instruments and anything else they could make more cheaply than workers at the assembly plants could. It did not take much skill or expensive machinery to assemble such cars.

Canadians did more than produce and sell cars; they also tried to control their consequences. By 1987, Alberta and Prince Edward Island had finally made seat belts compulsory. About the same time, luxury cars began to include a big airbag that inflated during a collision, protecting occupants from damage. The eighties also saw a crusade against an old problem: drunk drivers. Manitoba led the way with the toughest law: a police officer could impound the car and immediately suspend the licence of any driver who failed a breathalyzer test. Lawyers and some judges protested that such a law defied the right to a fair trial as guaranteed by Canada's new Charter of Rights and Freedoms. Others insisted that it was "reasonable" in a free and democratic society to take harsh action against a social menace. Judges generally supported the hard line and other provinces followed Manitoba's lead.

below: **In the 1980s, a growing number of people felt the dependability and quality of their cars were more important than style.**
Ford of Canada.

Cars are recycled into many unimaginable forms. From the grave-yard of cars, they are compressed and reshaped for many different uses. They could be made into rods (as shown in the warehouse inset photo) such as those used in the construction of the Skydome *(far right inset)* or other buildings.
Lasco Company

Lasco Company

Lasco Company

SEATBELTS ARE REQUIRED TO BE WORN

Every driver in Canada is required to wear a seatbelt while driving The legislation is a provincial concern and the following are the dates that each province and territory made it mandatory to wear seatbelts:

1976   Quebec , Ontario

1977   British Columbia, Saskatchewan

1982   Newfoundland

1983   New Brunswick

1984   Manitoba

1985   Nova Scotia

1987   Alberta

1988   Prince Edward Island

1990   Northwest Territories, Yukon

An alliance of law, improved design and safety features finally turned around the steady escalation of road accidents and fatalities. In 1970, there were 498 837 recorded vehicle accidents; ten years later, there were only 183 302. In 1970, there were 5080 fatalities and 5461 in 1980 but only 4360 in 1985 and 3685 in 1990. It was still too many, but the reduction — at a time when more cars than ever were on the roads, showed that highway tragedies were not inevitable.

Trade was a major issue of the 1980s. As a trading country, Canada feared that its exports would not only be shut out of a protectionist European Economic Community (EEC) and Japan but also shut out by the United States. Since Americans bought 80 percent of Canada's exports, that was terrifying. A Royal Commission, created to help plan Canada's economic future, recommended a free-trade deal with the United States. Almost all professional economists agreed. So did most of the Progressive Conservative delegates who chose Brian Mulroney as leader in 1983.

As prime minister, Mulroney soon discovered that good relations with the United States depended on getting along with President Ronald Reagan, who favoured a North American free trade area that would even include Mexico. And surely one proof that free trade could work was the renewed success of the Auto Trade Pact of 1965. The Pact had created jobs, profits and good working conditions in Canada — and Bob White's proud new union was part of the proof.

Not all Canadians agreed. They warned that Americans would gain even greater control of the Canadian economy through a free trade agreement, and that creating "a level playing field" between the two countries would soon flatten out the social programs that Americans lacked and Canadians financed through their taxes. Unionists, Bob White among them, warned that jobs and capital would move south, leaving Canada to provide Americans with raw materials at low prices. Business and finance and their friends in the Mulroney government rejected such warnings and insisted that Canada had no choice. In 1988, Canadians re-elected Brian Mulroney's government and the Canada-U.S. Free Trade Agreement was soon ratified. Unfortunately, the latter coincided with a new and even deeper recession — fresh trouble for car manufacturers, their dealers, suppliers and workers.

Safer, cleaner and more efficient than ever, cars and their by-products still caused trouble. Environmentalists claimed that each car sent a tonne of pollution into the atmosphere annually. A two-week fire at a tire dump at Hagersville in southern Ontario filled the sky with black smoke and soot. A year later, after United Nations forces liberated Kuwait from Iraqi invaders, the entire world's climate was affected by smoke from burning oil wells in the tiny oil-rich kingdom.

Surveys showed that most Canadians thought that people should take public transit and pay fines if their cars polluted. But that was for others. Voters resisted proposals that their own cars should be banned from crowded downtowns or that they should pay pollution and parking taxes. Were we hypocrites? And who cared? Hadn't critics labeled post-1945 babies the "Me" Generation?

In February 1990, a dump that held about 14 million tires caught fire in Hagersville, Ontario. It took firefighters 17 days to put it out, and clean up went on through the following year

Chrysler Canada

An interesting trend of the decade was the increasing popularity of trucks and vans for personal use — 23% of households owned at least one in 1987. Chrysler's "Magic Wagon," a boxy-looking family van, turned out to be the innovation of the 1980s, and it was made in Canada. The company took three months to transform its Windsor plant into the most advanced car factory of its time, with 125 robots to paint, weld and perform other jobs formerly done by humans. In 1984, Chrysler was Canada's eighth biggest company, with 12 000 production workers, $400 million in salaries and $6.3 billion in sales — and the rest of the auto industry was struggling to catch up.

In the 1980s, the auto industry finally began to give mobility to those who needed it most. In the wake of 1979, the Year of the Disabled, governments needed buses and vans to provide public transit for people in wheelchairs. The industry came up with hydraulic elevators to lift wheelchairs to floor level and buses that could "kneel" to ease entry for elderly or disabled passengers.

- Jean Chrétien and the Liberals crush the Conservatives, now led for the first time by a woman, Kim Campbell, in 1993.

- Canadians participate in United Nations peacemaking operations in Kuwait, Somalia, Bosnia and central Africa.

- Canadians face drastic cuts in health, education and other public services as governments cut spending to curb public deficits and debt.

- Overfishing of Atlantic cod and Pacific salmon forces Ottawa to shut down both fisheries.

- On October 30, 1995, Quebeckers narrowly vote to stay in Confederation, but separatists say they will win next time.

HIGHWAY 407

Ontario's ETR 407 Express Toll Route was built as a direct response to the population growth in the Greater Toronto Area and the inability of the existing highway system to meet the demand. In the past two decades, the number of licensed drivers in Ontario has almost doubled, and so has the number of registered vehicles. The state-of-the-art electronic toll collection system automatically records, by means of a "transponder," the beginning and end of the time each vehicle spends on the highway. Regular invoices are sent to ETR 407 users. For those cars without transponders, tolls and collected by a plate recognition system that generates mailed invoices.

Canadian Highways International Corporation

Canadian Highways International Corporation

CHAPTER TEN

1990-2000

SHARING THE PLANET WITH WHEELS

As the twentieth century lurched into its last decade, cars were as controversial as ever but no one seemed ready to give them up. By 1990, 86% of Canadians over the age 16 were licensed to drive, compared to only 78 % in 1979. In 1990, there were more cars, trucks and motorcycles on Canadian roads than ever before: 16.9 million. Most were driven farther too — an average of 17 380 kilometres or 2.7 times the width of Canada. But they did it on a lot less fuel — 2090 litres in 1988 compared to 2620 litres in 1980.

And the auto industry was as important as ever to the Canadian economy. If Canada was now the sixth largest auto producer in the world, and the industry contributed a quarter of Ontario's economic output. Making cars and their parts employed one manufacturing worker in six, and another 10 000 workers in the steel industry. Canadian cars consumed 19% of Canadian wire goods, nine % of glass products and six% of carpeting and fabrics. Canada's 3500 car dealers employ another 80 000 people. Canadian production provided the whole of mighty General Motors' profits in 1994 under its first Canadian president in thirty years, Maureen Darkes.

1997 Chrysler Neon
Chrysler Canada

PHOTO RADAR

When photo radar was introduced as a tool to nab speeders it met with mixed reviews. While proponents believed that photoradar saves lives and reduces health and insurance costs, critics charge that this traffic enforcement is mainly a cash grab and that driver education is the key solution.

As early as the 1970s, photo radar was considered in Quebec by the Montreal Police but without implementation. In 1997, Quebec allowed police to seize licences of suspected drunk drivers. In Ontario, photo radar was introduced by the provincial NDP government. There was a strong protest against it and in 1995, following an election, the new Conservative party scrapped the program. Alberta on the other hand, launched a sobering ad campaign with the message "Speed Kills" as added muscle to its photo radar program. British Columbia introduced the program in 1996, focusing on high-accident areas.

The average driving distance in 1990 was about 19 128 km a year.

In the 1990s, Canadians told their governments to cut deficits and taxes and to cut regulations, too. One way to cut costs was to sell publicly owned services and to persuade business to do the work governments had usually done. British Columbia led other provinces in contracting highway maintenance to private companies instead of using government workers. American governments had been building toll roads and bridges for years. To build Highway 407 north of Toronto, Ontario's government invited a private corporation to do the job. To cover costs and make a profit, users would have to pay tolls, and certainly some drivers would be willing to do so to avoid the congestion and potholes on public highways. Meanwhile, a Calgary company organized construction of a "Fixed Link," or combination bridge-causeway, from New Brunswick to Prince Edward Island, across the sometimes stormy and ice-packed 13 kilometres of the Northumberland Strait. It was opened on June 1, 1997, and was named "Confederation Bridge," and by using it cars and trucks would save 85 minutes of the time taken until then to cross by ferry. Drivers, not taxpayers, would pay for the construction through tolls.

left: **The 407 ETR is an all-electronic toll system. There are no toll booths to slow traffic. Most motorists use a transponder placed on their windshield. As they enter and exit the highway, their personal account information is read electronically and their account is automatically charged for the distance travelled.**
Canadian Highways International Corporation

below: **The combination land-water vehicle was a good idea in the 1960s. Naturally, it was not broadly popular, but in the 1990s it was again being manufactured. This one on land is one of these amazing cars, that just came out of the water where it was driven like a boat.**
Ken Pearson

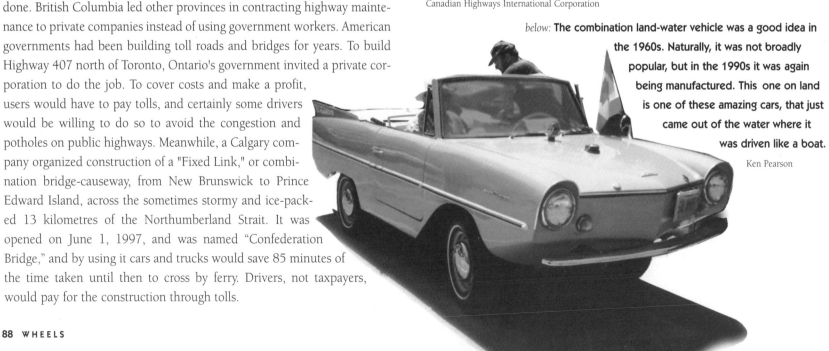

> Previously joined by ferry service, the Confederation Bridge opened on June 1, 1997, linking New Brunswick and Prince Edward Island, and thousands of people joined the celebrations by running across the mammoth bridge.
>
> Moncton Times & Transcript

Cars in the 1990s were mostly safer and more long-lasting than cars of earlier decades. Plastic bodies and bumpers did not rust or corrode. Micro-chips brought computer technology to anti-lock brakes and improved fuel economy. New aluminum alloys made engines last longer. Lighter cars went faster on a lot less gas. Cellular radios and telephones meant that drivers and passengers could always keep in touch. Soon there would be satellite navigation systems to end the "lost feeling" in the suburbs or countryside.

Hard times and better quality combined to persuade a lot of people to hang on to their family cars a lot longer. Marketing experts told automakers to focus on the special features that made one brand seem better than another. Other experts advised cutting prices by squeezing out the frills. Manufacturers certainly wanted to eliminate many of their own production jobs by "outsourcing" to smaller parts suppliers, many of which had lower wages, harsher working conditions and no union. Some were located in Mexico where workers had to accept much the same pay and conditions as Henry Ford had allowed in 1914. Still, Canada's autoworkers' union was able to protect its shrinking membership at a time when many other unions were in full retreat.

Employment in auto industry increased by 17% between 1983 and 1993. By 1993, 520,000 Canadians were employed in the auto industry. The average weekly payrolls for this industry were over $350 million.

In the mid-1990s, there were 13 782 service stations in Canada. Of these, well over four thousand combined full-serve and self-serve operations. They employed 75 000 people and created a further 1200 indirect jobs.

Chrysler Canada

AIR BAGS

Air bags in cars were introduced as a safety measure, but, unfortunately, they played a role in the deaths of four Canadians in car accidents between 1993 and 1997. After the United States announced that they would allow deactivation of some vehicle air bags in 1997, a similar announcement was made by Canadian authorities. The exceptions included people with medical problems; those who must put a child under 12 years of age in a front seat; people who must put a rear-facing child in the front passenger seat; those who must have driver's seat within 25.4 cm of the steering wheel.

MADD
CANADA ™
Mothers Against Drunk Driving

MADD (Mothers Against Drunk Drivers) Formed in 1990 as a women's action group against drunk drivers, MADD was soon amalgamated with PRIDE (People to Reduce Impaired Driving Everywhere). MADD has provided help to over 90 000 victims in Canada. The first woman president, Jane Meldrum, lost her son, Graham, 33, in 1990 when he was killed by an oncoming drunk driver who crossed a four-lane highway and struck his car.

Through a red ribbon campaign, MADD brings the message to avoid any situation in which there is drinking and driving. "Call a friend, have a designated driver come out with you, stay where you are, take public transportation, but do not drive with someone who has been drinking"

DRINKING AND DRIVING

It is a crime in Canada to drive a vehicle while impaired by alcohol or other drugs. Drunk driving is the largest single criminal cause of death and injury. In 1994, impaired driving was a contributing factor in 50 percent of all traffic fatalities, with drunk drivers killing three times more people than murderers.

Impaired driving is also the country's single most frequent Criminal Code Offence. In 1995, 59 percent of 172 437 Criminal Code traffic incidents reported by police across Canada involved driving while impaired. Like a murderer or bank robber, a convicted impaired driver has a criminal record.

In 1997, Quebec allowed police to seize licences of suspected drunk drivers.

GRADUATED LICENCES

Collisions are the leading cause of death for people between 16 and 24.

In 1994, Ontario introduced a system of graduated licencing as a means of reducing the risks faced by new, less experienced drivers. As a result of this experiment there was a dramatic drop in teenage traffic accidents and deaths. In two years, the number of accidental deaths involving 16-year-old drivers fell by more than half. British Columbia and Nova Scotia have introduced some restrictions on their new licences.

He didn't look like a murderer, my daughter's boyfriend Mike. But that's what he was! My daughter Lynn was only 21 when it happened. She thought she was in love and that it would last forever. But forever ended one Saturday night. They'd been at a friend's house, partying. Lynn had a drink or two, and her boyfriend had three beers. He didn't think three beers were enough to make him drunk. And it was just a short drive home anyway.

If I only knew then what I know now, I would have told Lynn to call a cab. Or to call me. Or even to walk. Anything. Anything but getting into the car with him when he'd been drinking. As they were driving in our neighbourhood, they went around the bend and a car pulled out of a hidden driveway. Mike wasn't as alert as he should have been and he didn't see the other car until the last moment...until it was too late. He tried to swerve. there was a crash he as fine! The other driver sustained a case of whiplash.

But my Lynn... You see, it was the passenger side that took the most impact. The passenger side... and Lynn. An ambulance arrived quickly, but it was not quick enough for my Lynn. She died en route to the hospital. When I got to the hospital, Mike told me what had happened. I literally wanted to kill him. What made it worse was how easy he got off. He lost his licence for a year, but that was it. I would have cheerfully given up my licence for life, if it meant I could get Lynn back. But she's not coming back. Ever. I wish that It was me that had died

We are now close to a new millennium. What will be in the next chapters of this book when it appears after the year 2000? Will we rediscover the energy crisis of the 1970s? Will we build more roads with systems of "user pay"? Some European countries have electronic sensors that identify cars and bill their owners for the kilometres driven. Ontario's new toll highways have a similar system. Will this be how future roads will be paid for? Will there be major styling changes and new safety features? What would you like to see in the car you might buy in the year 2001? Or should we even want our own personal "wheels"? Do cars cost our stressed-out planet too much? Would our cities be better if more people shared public transit? Canada's literary phrase-maker, the late Marshall McLuhan, claimed that wheels were as obsolete in the electronic age as penmanship had become in the age of typesetting. With the Internet, who needs to drive over for a visit?

Whatever happens, "wheels" will probably still matter in our lives. They and the roads and services they need create jobs for millions of Canadians. They shape our cities and our countryside. They give us a freedom of movement others can only envy. Still, no pleasure is without a price, and more and more of us are wondering what we can afford.

Books end; history doesn't.

Robotics are now a part of the assembly of the automobile. At the turn of the 19th century Ford of Canada produced an automobile every 14 hours. With the introduction of mass production in 1913, production time was cut dramatically to just 93 minutes per vehicle. By the end of the century the assembly line capacity was 75 cars per hour or one car every 48 seconds. Ford of Canada.

Transplants (Asian-owned automobile assembly plants) have had a significant effect on North America automobile industry. In 1992 transplants represented 16% of all automobiles built in Canada.

photo: Toyota Canada

inset: **Ford Canada's highly automated paint facility uses 23 painting robots to paint 88 Windstar minivans per hour.**

Ford of Canada.

opposite page: **In the age of automation, the familiar command "fillerup" was often answered by the driver, getting out in the cold, heat, snow or rain to fill the tank from an automated pump. A major source of jobs for generations of young people faded fast.**

Imperial Oil

below: **Does the future lie with the electric car? Here is the GM Electric Vehicle Prototype Impact.** General Motors of Canada

The automobile industry is the largest manufacturing sector and contributes more to Canadian exports than any other industry.

THE HUNT FOR A ZERO-EMISSION ENGINE

Ever since cars have been manufactured widely, fossil fuel in the form of gasoline has been used for energy. Environmental concerns have motivated a relentless search for alternative, environmentally friendly and commercially viable fuels. This search has ranged from electric power to fuel-cell technology to many less practical considerations.

In Canada, Ballard Power Systems has pioneered the process of converting hydrogen to electricity without combustion from sources such as methanol, natural gas and even gasoline. By the end of the 1990s, Ballard was testing its new technology, the Ballard Fuel Cell, in buses in Vancouver and Chicago. They are working with major automobile companies to develop zero-emission for commercial vehicles by early in the 21st century.

SELECTED EVENTS IN CANADIAN AUTOMOBILE HISTORY

1867 The oldest known surviving Canadian-built car, a steam buggy, is built by Henry Seth Taylor of Stanstead, Quebec.

Robert McLaughlin establishes a carriage-making business in Enniskillen, Ontario. In 1878 he moves the business to Oshawa, and in 1907 his sons negotiate for the sole right to manufacture Buick cars in Canada.

1883 Canada's first electric car is built, marking the transition from wagon steam carriages to the concept of the modern automobile. It is built by Frederick Featherstonhaugh and William Still, who designed the car's batteries and motor.

1895 George Foss of Sherbrooke, Quebec, builds a one-cylinder gas car and drives it for four years.

1897 The Tudhope Carriage Company is formed in Orillia, Ontario, and remains active until the 1920s. The company builds the Tudhope-McIntyre, a reliable, easy-starting vehicle, and the first truck ever owned by the Bell Telephone Company of Canada.

William Still is backed by the Canadian Motor Syndicate to develop a storage battery to drive a carriage.

1899 The LeRoy is Canada's first production-model automobile assembled in Kitchener, Ontario. Unfortunately, it has no brakes. Instead, you stop the car by reversing gear.

The first self-propelled vehicle is assembled in the West, in Vancouver.

A two-seater, called an Ivanhoe, is built by William Gray & Sons and is put on display at the Canadian National Exhibition in Toronto.

1899 The first motorized delivery wagon made in Canada, the Still Electric, is used by Parker Dye Works of Toronto.

1900 The original McLaughlin factory burns to the ground and the town of Oshawa offers a $50 000 loan, "payable when convenient," convincing the McLaughlins to stay there. In 1907 the first McLaughlin car, a Model F, is built – a two-cylinder, 22 hp touring car with a red chassis and dark wine body. It costs $1400, including horn and gas headlights but no top or windshield.

D. A. Maxwell of Waterford, Ontario, builds a gas buggy that runs for 24 years.

Canada's first automobile accident is recorded on May 1 in Winnipeg between a horse and a car.

1901 Queen City Cycle and Motor Works of Toronto builds the Queen gas buggy, but the company folds in 1903.

1902 George Foss builds the first Canadian gasoline automobile.

1903 Ontario is the first province to license motor vehicles. The cost is $2.00 per vehicle. The speed limit is 10 mph (16 km/h) in the cities and towns and 15 mph (24km/h) in the country. To alert their coming, drivers are given the choice of using a bell, a horn or even a gong.

1904 The Ford Motor Company begins operation in the former Walkerville Wagon Works in Windsor, Ontario. Receiving its charter on August 17, it starts assembling cars on October 10. In the first year, 117 cars are built. Gordon McGregor, president of the Walkerville Wagon company, decides that the automobile is the wave of the future and he contracts Henry Ford in the United States to build the cars. The Ford Motor Company is incorporated on August 17, 1904.

CCM stages its own auto show in Toronto, displaying the Ivanhoe and other makes it sells.

Regular speed races are held in Winnipeg at the Industrial Exhibition.

1905 The Russell Motor Car Company is formed as a subsidiary of the Canada Cycle and Motor Company (CCM) of Toronto. The Russell becomes the pre-eminent Canadian car before WWI, but production ceases in 1915.

1906 The Tudhope Motor Company of Orillia, Ontario, which had built horse-drawn carriages since the 1860s, decides to motorize some of its products. After a fire in 1909 it builds the Everitt, a 4-cylinder car. In 1913 the company name is changed to the Fisher Motor Company, but it ceases manufacture after the First World War.

Chatham Motor Company is formed and builds the Chatham, a sold reliable car with elegant, curved bodywork.

Montreal's first automobile show opens April 21.

McCulloch and Boswell, Winnipeg automobile dealers, build a car with an engine that is water-cooled in summer and air-cooled in winter.

1907 The first gas filling station in Canada opens in Vancouver.

1908 After the formation of General Motors Company, the first McLaughlin appears and the McLaughlin Carriage Company produces 200 cars.

The Ford Model T, the "Universal Car", is introduced and changes the auto industry.

Formal car racing begins in Montreal, with a three-day meet. It draws 10 000 people.

1909 The Model T is introduced and sells for $1150.

The two-cylinder Reo is built in Canada by the Reo Motor Company in St. Catharines, Ontario. In 1922 Reo builds the first Canadian "camper," a six-cylinder car with a special rear section.

McLaughlin initiates the first hand-operated windshield wiper.

1910 The gasoline car evolves into the form that prevails to this day.

Electric lights appear on cars

1911 Manitoba and New Brunswick issue licence plates. Alberta and Saskatchewan begin in 1912 and British Columbia in 1913, Nova Scotia in 1918 and Yukon in 1923.

Leaving the east coast on August 27, Thomas W. Wilby, from Great Britain, becomes the first man to cross Canada coast to coast with a car. He can't drive all the way as a transcontinental road is only a dream, so he uses trains and other means as well. By the end of his trip, some 4200 miles (6700 km) are registered on the odometer.

The first power windshield wiper is introduced.

1912 The cost of a tire averages $50, making it one of the most expensive parts of a car.

The electric self-starter is introduced.

1913 The T. Eaton Company begins selling cars by mail-order catalogue. The company even puts the cars in their showrooms and gives the usual guarantee of satisfaction or money returned.

1915 The Ford Motor Company voluntarily raises wages of employees to $4 a day and reduces the work week to 48 hours.

Chevrolet Motor Company of Canada is established in Oshawa, Ontario.

1918 General Motors of Canada is formed when "Mr. Sam" McLaughlin sells the McLaughlin Motor Car Company to General Motors in the U.S. Oshawa is selected as the home of the entire General Motors line.

Joseph Lavoie of Montreal begins work on the Lavoie car. He creates one of the first V-6 engines.

The McLaughlin and Canadian Chevrolet companies merge to form General Motors of Canada, with R. S. McLaughlin as president.

1919 Canada's first national Highway Act is passed, providing funds to the provinces to build and maintain roads.

General Motors introduces its first trucks built in Canada.

1920 The first adjustable seat is introduced.

1921 The stop light is introduced in cars.

Winnipeg Motor Cars Limited is incorporated by Frank and Dave Ogletree, E. Herbert, and Louis Arsenault with the slogan "As good as wheat."

1992 On January 1, British Columbia is the last province in Canada to change to driving on the right-hand side of the road. Alberta had switched in 1921.

1924 Dodge Motors begins manufacturing in Walkerville, Ontario, and eventually becomes the Chrysler Corporation of Canada.

1925 Chrysler Corporation of Canada is incorporated and three years later it acquires Dodge Brothers and Graham Brothers.

Dr. P. E Doolittle, Canadian Automobile Company, and Edward Flickenger, Ford Motor Company, drive a Ford Model T from the Halifax to Vancouver entirely on Canadian soil. The trip takes from September 8 to October 17, and some 500 miles (800km) the car is put on trains as roads don't exist or are unusable.

1926 The Model T Ford has its best sales year, in what turns out to be the last full year of its production.

1929 Chrysler opens a new car assembly plant outside Windsor, Ontario. The first Dodge truck is made there in 1931.

The first car is produced by General Motors at their Regina plant.

1930s Hydraulic brakes are introduced.

1931 Hudson-Essex of Canada Limited of Tilbury, Ontario, is incorporated on December 30. They manufacture the Hudson, a sturdy car that gains a fine reputation. The Nash Motors of Canada Canadian branch plant is set up in

1946. Finally, in 1956, American Motors Sales (Canada) is formed from these beginnings.

1932 Ford introduces the first car powered by its soon-to-be famous V-8 engine.

1931-33 The Frontenac is the last Canadian-only built car. The American parent company from which it evolved was Durant Motors. In its first two years the company produces over 13 000 Stars and Durants from its factory in Leaside, Ontario. Unable to expand sales outside Ontario, it closes in 1935.

1934 Chrysler introduces a one-piece curved windshield.

1936 The Canadian government reduces tariffs to $17\frac{1}{2}\%$ on all cars and trucks, except those from British Empire countries, which are free of tariff. These measures require that 60% of the cost of production be Canadian or British Empire labour and materials. As a result, Studebaker, Hudson and Packard motor companies cannot meet these requirements and cease production in Canada.

1937 Workers at Oshawa's General Motors plant strike for recognition of their union, Local 222 of the United Auto Workers.

1939 The Queen Elizabeth Way, the first four-lane, limited-access highway in North America, opens between Toronto and Hamilton

1939-1945 During the Second World War, the manufacture of civilian cars is suspended.

1943 On June 19, the 500 000th unit of Canadian-made motorized military equipment is delivered.

1945 A major automotive strike takes place at the Ford plant in Windsor. Workers insist on the right to have the company "check off" union dues and pay them directly to the union. Mr. Justice Rand in 1946 establishes a formula for union security: all workers pay dues for the costs of union representation but they don't have to join.

1946 The Nash Motor Company, predecessor of American Motors of Canada begins production in Toronto.

With peace-time production of cars resuming in 1946, Ford of Canada introduces the Monarch model, which is sold only in Canada.

1948 The Studebaker car begins manufacture in Hamilton, Ontario. The American company soon takes over the Packard Motor Company and in 1955 the name of the Canadian company is changed to Studebaker Packard Company of Canada. In 1963 the U.S. company stops production of the car and announces that the Hamilton factory will build Studebakers for the world. On March 4, 1966, the Hamilton factory is closed, signalling the end of Studebaker.

1956 American Motors Corporation is formed to sell Nash and Hudson cars in Canada. It incorporates the Hudson-Essex of Canada Limited and Nash Motors of Canada Limited.

1961 Dean Vincent W. Bladen issues his report on the Canadian automobile industry, recommending restoring import duty on British-made cars and remove excise tax on Canadian-made cars. When adopted this gave impetus to Canadian manufacturing industry.

1965 The Canada-U.S. Automotive Products Agreement ("Autopact"), integrating the auto industries in both countries, is introduced. By this agreement, companies that produce half or more of their vehicles in Canada and the U.S. can freely ship vehicles and parts across the border.

1967 The first Canadian Grand Prix for Formula One cars is held at Mosport Park, Ontario.

1968 Shoulder harnesses become standard equipment in passenger cars.

Exhaust emission control devices are included in most passenger cars.

1969 Manitoba introduces the first provincial-government-run car insurance program.

1971 The Trans-Canada Highway is completed, covering nearly 8 000 kilometres from coast to coast.

1972 Born in 1871, "Mr. Sam" McLaughlin, founder of the McLaughlin Motor Company and later General Motors of Canada dies on January 6, 1972.

1974 British Columbia introduces government-run automobile insurance.

1976 Quebec and Ontario are the first provinces to make wearing seatbelts mandatory.

1984 After rejecting concessions accepted by US members of the United Auto Workers, Bob White wins a strike against General Motors, breaks with the UAW and forms the Canadian Auto Workers (CAW). It is soon one of Canada's biggest unions.

1985 The federal government regulates exhaust emissions of hydrocarbons, carbon monoxide and oxides of nitrogen in Canadian manufactured automobiles.

1986 In November, the first car manufactured by Honda of Canada comes off the production line at the company's Alliston, Ontario plant.

1994 Graduated licensing, requiring a two-year program to obtain a driving licence, begins in Ontario.

1996 The Canadian Auto Workers Union reaches over 200 000 members. Although membership includes other industries, some 40% of the membership is from the auto industry.

1997 On June 1, the Confederation Bridge is opened, linking New Brunswick and Prince Edward Island.

1998 To reduce accidents caused by faulty commercial vehicles, Ontario introduces the impoundment of trucks and buses found to have critical defects.